Holy Lands
Reviving Pluralism
in the Middle East

COLUMBIA GLOBAL REPORTS
NEW YORK

Holy Lands
Reviving Pluralism in the Middle East

Nicolas Pelham

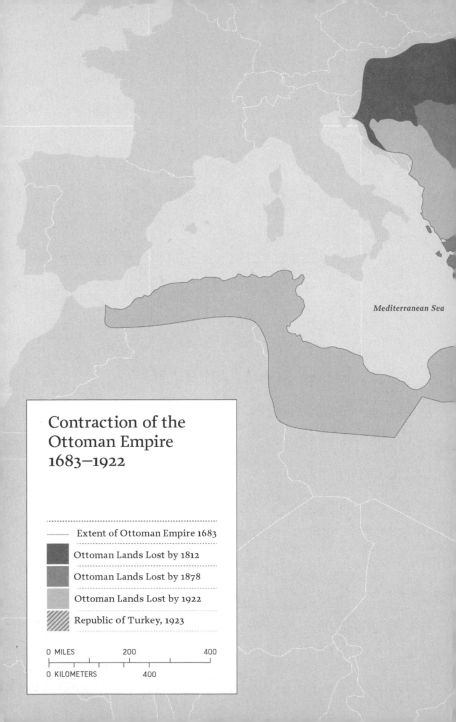

Mediterranean Sea

Contraction of the Ottoman Empire 1683–1922

....
— Extent of Ottoman Empire 1683
....
Ottoman Lands Lost by 1812
....
Ottoman Lands Lost by 1878
....
Ottoman Lands Lost by 1922
....
Republic of Turkey, 1923

0 MILES   200   400

0 KILOMETERS   400

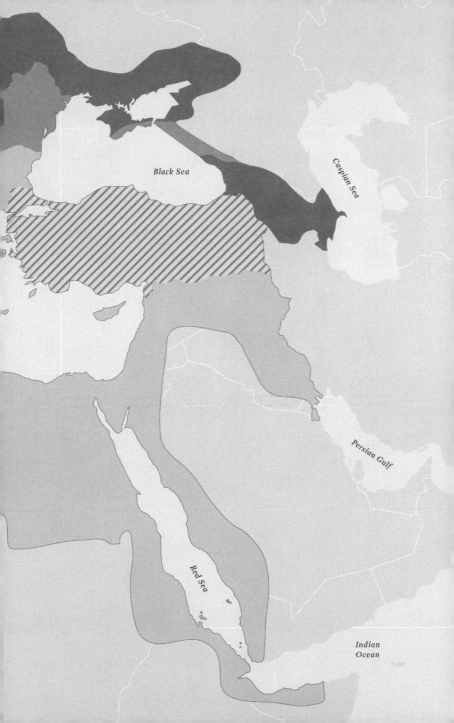

Black Sea

Caspian Sea

Persian Gulf

Red Sea

Indian Ocean

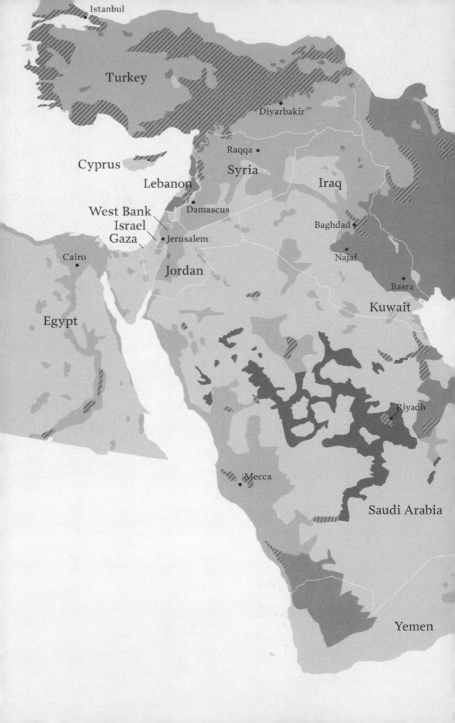

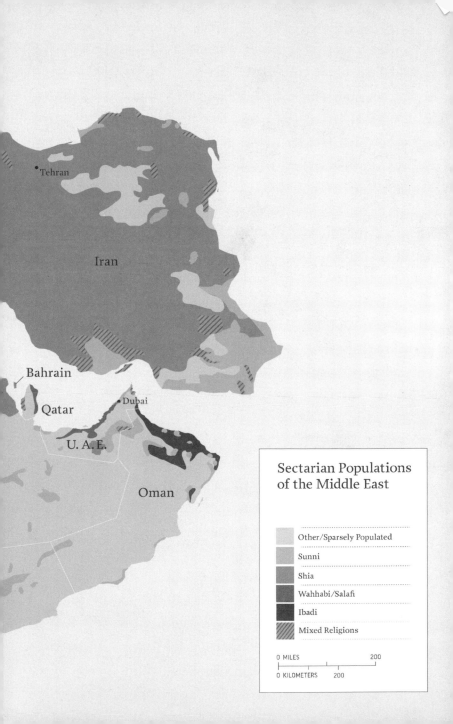

Sectarian Populations
of the Middle East

Other/Sparsely Populated

Sunni

Shia

Wahhabi/Salafi

Ibadi

Mixed Religions

0 MILES   200

0 KILOMETERS   200

Holy Lands:
Reviving Pluralism in the Middle East
Copyright © 2016 by Nicolas Pelham
All rights reserved

Published by Columbia Global Reports
91 Claremont Avenue, Suite 515
New York, NY 10027
globalreports.columbia.edu
facebook.com/columbiaglobalreports
@columbiaGR

Library of Congress Control Number:
2015949787
ISBN:
978-09909763-4-9

Book design by Strick&Williams
Map design by Jeffrey L. Ward
Author photograph by Lipika Pelham

Printed in the United States of America

CONTENTS

12   CAST OF CHARACTERS

Mustafa Kemal Atatürk
First president of Turkey, 1923–38

Recep Tayyip Erdoğan
President of Turkey, 2014–current

Ara Sarafian
British-Armenian historian of
the Armenian genocide

David Ben-Gurion
First prime minister of Israel,
1955–63

Benjamin Netanyahu
Current prime minister of Israel

Ilan Shohat
Mayor of Safed

Yona Yahav
Mayor of Haifa

Shimon Gafsou
Mayor of Nazareth Illit

Haviva Aranyi
Holocaust survivor

Yehuda Bauer
Israeli historian of the Holocaust

Muhammad ibn Abd al-Wahhab
Arabian founder of Wahhabism/
Salafism

Izz ad-Din al-Qassam
Syrian cleric and an architect
of modern Sunni jihadism

Abdullah Azzam
Palestinian cleric and founding
member of al-Qaeda

Osama bin Laden
Arabian founder of al-Qaeda

Abu Qatada al-Filistini
Jordanian leader of
Palestinian jihadism

Abu Muhammad al-Maqdisi
Jordanian-Palestinian spiritual
mentor of Abu Musab al-Zarqawi

Abu Musab al-Zarqawi
Jordanian founder of al-Qaeda
in Iraq/the Islamic State

Abu Bakr al-Baghdadi
Iraqi leader of the Islamic State

Muqtada al-Sadr
Iraqi leader of the Sadrist Movement

Saddam Hussein
President of Iraq, 1979–2003

Nouri al-Maliki
Prime minister of Iraq, 2006–14

Haider al-Abadi
Prime minister of Iraq,
2014–current

Ali Sistani
Leading grand ayatollah in Najaf

Abu Jaafar al-Darraji
Senior commander of the Badr
Organization

Mohammed Dahlan
Palestinian politician, security
advisor to Abu Dhabi crown prince

Mansour Malik
Founder, Islamic Law Chambers

Sayyid Abu Musameh
Former leader of Hamas in Gaza

Preface

Like many before me, my career in the Middle East was born of the thrill of the region's diversity. In Damascus, where I studied Arabic in the 1990s, going to different places of worship was as natural as a stroll in the park. Mornings might take in a synagogue service, lunchtimes an Orthodox mass, evenings the *salah* prayer at Ibn Taymiya's mosque, followed by a late-night *hammam*, a Turkish bath. Faith was theatrical, spectacular, wholesome, and uplifting.

It feels a lost world. At work, my reporting is limited ever more to the dreary cycle of violence. Instead of covering the region's vibrancy and creativity, most of my articles describe its demise. "More than 100,000 killed in one of Middle East's bloodiest years," was the headline with which the *Financial Times* rang in the New Year in 2015. None of the conflicts it listed—in Syria, Iraq, Israel and Palestine, Yemen, and Libya—showed any sign of waning, let alone ending. With each article, one's admiration for the region turns that bit more into pity.

This book is born of the gnawing question of how a region that for half a millennium was a global exemplar of pluralism and religious harmony has become the least tolerant and stable place on the planet. Through six essays from the field, the book explores the causes of the decline, and offers a few pointers for a recovery. Those hoping for a prescriptive template for resolving the Middle East's multiple crises will be disappointed. What they will find is a fresh approach for examining what has gone wrong, and perhaps a paradigm for understanding what might put it right.

In 1923, a Norwegian arctic explorer, Nobel Peace Prize winner, and the first League of Nations High Commissioner for Refugees, Fridtjof Nansen, devised a mass population exchange that became known as the Lausanne Convention. "Unmixing the populations of the Near East will tend to secure true pacification of the Near East," he reasoned. Building on the Wilsonian principles of national self-determination, his convention wound up the last vestiges of the Ottoman Empire in southeastern Europe after six centuries of religious co-existence. It provided for the "compulsory exchange of Turkish nationals of the Greek Orthodox religion established in Turkish territory, and of Greek nationals of the Moslem religion established in Greek territory." In the months that followed, 1.6 million people were displaced across the dying empire, many from communities that had never seen sectarian conflict.

18   Forcible population transfer was not a novel phenomenon. Encouraged by Europe's Christian great powers, for almost a century Christian nationalist movements had sloughed off Ottoman rule in southeastern Europe and purged their countries of their Muslim past. Russia, Bulgaria, Macedonia, and Greece killed and expelled hundreds of thousands of Muslims, as if revisiting Spain's Reconquista on southeastern Europe. But Nansen was the first to achieve diplomatically what others had achieved by war, and give the transformation of the Ottoman Empire's heterogeneous society into homogeneous societies an international stamp of approval. George Curzon, who as Britain's foreign secretary was one of the key negotiators, hailed "the advantages which would ultimately accrue to both countries from a greater homogeneity of population," and set about unmixing and partitioning Britain's other colonies along similar lines. The British government partitioned first Jerusalem—in which under Ottoman rule Muslims, Christians, and Jews all mingled together—into separate religious quarters, and then Palestine itself.

Communal segregation had ancient roots. From the outset, Ottoman sultans had administered their diverse empire on sectarian lines, devolving authority to the leaders of their multiple faith communities, or millets. Patriarchs, chief rabbis, and Muslim clerics headed semi-autonomous theocracies that applied religious laws. But while the millets governed their respective co-religionists, they had no power over land. The empire's many millets shared the same towns and villages with other millets. There were no ghettoes or confessional enclaves. Territorially, the powers of their respective leaders overlapped. I have called this system of overlapping religious powers milletocracy.

The unmixing of sects that the Lausanne Convention propagated in the Near East triggered a century of wars designed to turn holy communities into holy lands. Millet fought and evicted millet in the struggle to create gerrymandered enclaves that turned religious minorities into majorities. Across the region, a heterogeneous population was subject to attempts to sift, order, and refashion it as a patchwork of homogeneous ones. Far from delivering the pacification Nansen promised, the process has resulted in an ongoing program of secticide, or milleticide, which, as the *Financial Times*'s stark headline recorded, has only intensified over time.

Where religion under the Ottomans had been inclusive and at ease side by side other faiths, boxed inside borders its xenophobic and intolerant traits came to the fore. The faith community acquired the attributes and trappings of a nation-state. Defense of the land took precedence over universal values. Service in the military became the supreme expression of loyalty to the community. The new leaders, who were generals, not men of religion, highlighted the martial, nationalist, and exclusive aspects of their tradition. Some dismissed religious precepts altogether and fashioned a secular sectarianism. The millets of the Ottoman Empire mutated into truncated land cults that regarded other millets suspiciously as existential challenges.

Thus transformed, the region's millets proved as ruthless as contemporary jihadis. The generals of the Young Turks

20   eradicated the Armenian millet in Eastern Anatolia and the
      Greek Orthodox millet in the west. Jewish nationalists extir-
      pated 85 percent of Palestine's Muslim millet, and then erased
      their memory by relandscaping what for centuries had been a
      multi-cultural land. Arab nationalist leaders in return expelled
      all but a smattering of their ancient Jewish millet. In the latest
      chapter of milleticide, the Islamic State has homogenized the
      core of the region whose mosaic of Yazidis, Assyrian Christians,
      and Shia Muslims Islam had preserved for 1,400 years.

      Holy Lands explores the prospects for countering the territo-
      rial exclusivism that has seeped in from Europe and reviving
      the region's indigenous norms. Rather than look to external
      mechanisms for conflict resolution, it seeks to find remedies
      innate to the region. The first part maps the transition from
      Ottoman multi-culturalism to the mono-culturalism of the
      Turkish republic. Parts Two and Four are case studies of how
      traditionally quietest religious communities unaccustomed
      to power—Jews and Arab Shias—dealt with their newfound
      majority status. Part Three traces the response of the region's
      Sunnis to their relegation to minority status. Part Five explores
      the prospects for sectarian war region-wide.
          The final part asks whether a return to milletocracy
      might prove a better mechanism for balancing the interests
      of the region's multiple millets than the current battles over
      borders. For over half a millennium such a system kept the
      peace, and created a stable symbiosis in which all sects were
      stakeholders. By decoupling the rule of the sect from the
      rule of land, the region's bloodied millets might find an exit

strategy from secticide and restore their tarnished universal-
ism. Milletocracy might yet offer a paradigm for reviving the
region's rich tradition of pluralism and respect for diversity—
values so distant today.

Baghdad, October 2015

The Decline and Fall of the Ottoman Empire

Part One

The Origin of Milleticide

"God changes not what is in a people until they change what is
in themselves."
—Quran 13:11

A century or so ago, before armies and dams interrupted its
passage, a boat down the Tigris River would have sailed past the
holy places of the many sects that the river had nurtured and
harbored over thousands of years.

Near its source in the snowcapped peaks above the city
of Hakkâri, it would have floated speedily past bell towers of
Assyrian Christian churches, the El Rizk Mosque precariously
perched on Hasankeyf's cave-pocked cliffs, Armenian mon-
asteries with squat spires, and the lean finger of a minaret of
the eleventh-century Ulu Mosque, reputedly the fifth holiest
place in Islam, poking above Diyarbakır's brooding basalt walls.

24   It would meander past the Alevis' domed *cemevis,* or houses of gathering, and the caravans of the Yazidi pilgrims ascending to the mountain village of Lalish to visit the shrine of their peacock god, Melek Taus.

Approaching Mosul, the sun might have set over the thirteenth-century conical dome of Mashhad Yahya Abul Kassem and the stepped shrine of Jonah the Prophet. As the river swelled, fed by its tributaries, so too would the size of its holy places. Downriver, Samarra's golden al-Askari Shrine, resting place of the tenth and eleventh Shia imams, would have glimmered on the horizon, and like sentries at the gates, the Shia shrine of Kadhimiya and the Sunni shrine of Abu Hanifa would have watched over the traffic heading into Baghdad from opposite banks of the river. Beyond lay the Jewish tomb of Ezra the high priest, and the Mandi temples of the Sabeans, who robed in white tunics and baptized themselves in its waters in honor of John the Baptist, their true prophet. Finally, weighed by watering thousands of years of traditions, the Tigris would merge with the Euphrates to form the sluggish, aging Shatt al-Arab and relieve itself of the burden, spilling into the Persian Gulf.

In the late spring of 1915, at a turn in the Tigris downstream from Diyarbakır, the idyll came to an end. Turkish gendarmes moored their *keleks*—rafts made of bloated goatskins covered in reeds—at the mouth of a dry ravine, offloaded their cargo of 600 shackled Armenian notables, and handed them over to Kurdish tribesmen for disposal. There can be few more scenic sites for a massacre. Hawks darted over the grassy hilltops mocking the passivity of the victims between the cliffs. According to local folklore, the Armenians stayed stoically still, resigned to the head-chopping. The blood of the elders was said to be black from all the cigarettes they had smoked. Bystanders cut open the corpses, scavenging for gold the Armenians might have swallowed before they were led away.

No one has erected a plaque to mark the massacre, and soon it will be hard to find. The site is slated to be submerged by a new Turkish dam. The erasure of Anatolia's Armenians, once a tenth of the local population, will be complete.

Downstream in the Iraqi city of Mosul, the jihadi forces of the Islamic State a century or so later inaugurated their caliphate with a similar exercise in cultural homogenization. As Armenians before them, shackled Yazidi men passively submitted to throat-slitting. Their women and girls were farmed out as sex trophies or sold in markets as slaves. Some of the perpetrators, though separated by a century, were even related. A large number of IS fighters were descendants of the Muslim Circassians and Chechens of Khabur, who had been expelled from Tsarist Russia over the course of the nineteenth century, and in 1915 took revenge by preying on Assyrian and Armenian Christians as they marched through Syria's desert. The priests at Baghdad's Assyrian Church of St. Peter use the term *sayfo*, Syriac for sword, for the massacres then and now. The *Daily Mail*, a popular and influential British tabloid, speaks for many when it traces the thread connecting the two to the "blood-soaked depravity" of Islam.

They are mistaken. The Armenian genocide was the brainchild not of religious clerics but of largely secular generals who revolted against them. The Turkish nationalists who

26   took their inspiration from European nationalists who rose up against the Ottoman Empire's reactionary emperors and turned the caliphate into a republic. In the name of Westernization, they closed the country's Sufi lodges and legislated against the display of religious symbols in government buildings, including the veil and the fez. They gutted Ottoman Turkish of its Arabic, Persian, and Kurdish implants as ruthlessly as they cleansed populations.

The Islamic system that was overthrown had a centuries-old record of pluralism that for most of its tenure was unmatched by Christendom. Though the Black Death ravaged the Middle East as mercilessly as Europe, the Muslim religious establishment, unlike the Christian, did not blame Jews for poisoning the wells. And when Christian Europe initiated inquisitions, *autos-da-fé*, expulsions, and forced conversions to root out pagans, heretics, and Jews, the Ottoman Empire offered a refuge—the very reverse of the migration patterns seen today. Even Christians fleeing Western Europe's wars of religion found sanctuary, earning it the sobriquet *La Convivencia*, a place of co-existence. "The asylum of the universe," was how Francis I addressed the caliphate after his capture by Charles V at the Battle of Pavia in 1525. God had created many peoples to know each other, said the Quran, not to fight. St. James, Spain's patron saint, by contrast, is still affectionately known as Matamoros, Muslim killer.

Old Ottoman Pluralism

Long before Britain, France, or the United States conquered the world, Ottoman rule epitomized globalization. Its empire stretched from Belgrade to Basra, smudging the contours between East and West and leaving them less defined than they are today.

The empire was open to outsiders. From the sixteenth century, foreigners made up an increasingly influential segment of Ottoman rule. They were entrusted to run their own affairs, under a system of capitulations that exempted them from sharia law, dress codes, and taxes. In the process, the ports they supervised evolved into *entrepôts*, or international trading hubs. Seventeenth-century Europeans away from their wives found Istanbul, with its license for temporary marriages, a libertine place to be.

The Ottoman Empire's pluralism proved remarkably resilient, despite the erosion at its edges and the predatory

28 designs of other colonial powers. On the eve of the First World
War while fighting the Balkan wars, Anatolia's four million
Greeks and Armenians were opening and upgrading churches.
Now hidden by a phalanx of department stores, an Armenian
church, Üç Horan, with imposing Corinthian columns, loomed
over Istanbul's main thoroughfare, İstiklâl Caddesi. A short
distance away lay the Armenian cemetery, which the republic
later levelled and turned into central Istanbul's Taksim Square.
Armenians filled the upper ranks of the civil service and banks.

Sultan Abdülhamid II's foreign minister for most of
his reign was an Armenian, as was Lebanon's governor and
the prime minister in Egypt (who oversaw construction of
the Suez Canal). The Duzian family ran the Imperial Mint,
the Balyans designed his palaces, and the Dadians ran the
imperial armories and gunpowder mills. Together with Greeks
and Jews, Armenians comprised 60 percent of the staff of the
Ottoman Imperial Bank, the empire's central bank. For safekeeping, Muslim generals would leave their wives in Armenian
care before embarking on campaigns.

Such was the level of integration that the Ottomans had
no word for minorities. (The Arabic term *aqaliyat* is a late
nineteenth-century invention.) Had there been one, Muslims
would have been counted amongst them, since even after a
thousand years of Islam, Muslims comprised some 40 percent
of the empire's subjects. The percentage of Turks would have
been far smaller. But rather than establish an ethnic hierarchy,
the Ottomans ruled by devolving power to the millet, or religious community, of which it counted some 17, Islam included.
Each millet was semi-autonomous, administering its own

co-religionists, raising its own taxes, and applying and enforcing its own religious laws. Subjects regardless of creed could
petition the sultan directly, turning him into a quasi-court of
appeal, but on day-to-day matters the millet determined the
affairs of its denomination.

When Europe was locking in ghettoes what minorities it
had not annihilated, Islamic scribes recount how on their holy
days Christian patriarchs and Jewish dignitaries led their flocks
through the Middle East's cities dressed in finery that rivaled
that of the caliph. Istanbul was an Armenian and Orthodox
capital as well as an Islamic one. Europe took centuries to learn
such tolerance. Only in 1926, almost a century after its conquest
of Algeria, did Paris authorize the opening of France's first
mosque.

Yet far from castigating Europe's culture, as the current
pretender of Islamic State does, the Ottoman caliphs patronized
it. Abdülhamid II had his underwear tailored in Paris, and not only
built his own opera house but sang in it, repeatedly hosting Sarah
Bernhardt, the society actress of her day. His orchestra played
Verdi in the streets on his return from the mosque. European
architects, painters, and composers, including the brother of
Gaetano Donizetti, flocked to their courts. The last caliph,
Abdülmecid II, performed the violin at weekly palace concerts
attended by men and women. The women in his paintings,
including his wife, Şehsuvar Kadınefendi, read Goethe's *Faust*.

Non-Muslim subjects of the empire frequently went court-
shopping, comparing their own religious laws with those in
sharia courts or secular ones, and selecting whichever offered
more rights. Sharia courts proved particularly attractive for

30   Catholic and Jewish women, whose own legal codes did not sanction a woman's right to divorce. Many adopted a similarly eclectic approach to religious rites, frequenting each other's saints' days and holy men and women. Muslim doctors whispered Quranic verses to the Christian babies they delivered, and Muslims carried amulets inscribed with Gospel sayings.

Popular inter-faith culture was officially sanctioned. A modern highway zips past Sisli's Darülaceze, the retirement home Abdülhamid II built in 1896, above Istanbul's Golden Horn. Cars go too fast for passengers to catch the golden Arabic herald over the mahogany doors. But for those who take time to stop, the long courtyard shaded with cypress trees offers not just an escape from modern Istanbul's frenzy but a time capsule showcasing caliphal values. At either end of the courtyard he erected three places of worship: a mosque to the south, a church and a synagogue to its north. Contemporary interpreters of the Quran claim Islam bans the building of new non-Muslim places of worship. But even as Orthodox Christians and Zionists were seeking to oust the Ottomans and rule themselves, the caliph was still building holy places for his multi-faith subjects.

The pluralism was not egalitarian. Until abolition in the mid-nineteenth century, Ottoman manpower depended heavily on slave tributes, in which Christian boys predominantly from the rural Balkans were dragooned into the sultan's army, sulphur factories, and courts as *ghulam*, or sodomites. It was pernicious, but for some the practice was a fast track to aggrandizement and leverage at the pinnacle of power. As conscripts and concubines, slaves formed the military, the nobility, and the mothers of the new sultans. From the lowliest captive, a slave girl could rise to the most powerful person in the empire; an Albanian guttersnipe could become a grand vizier.

The status of non-Muslims as *dhimmis*, or protected persons, also detracted from the equality of the millet system. On paper and in some districts and at some times, non-Muslims could not testify in sharia courts, wore distinguishing costumes until the late eighteenth century, and were prohibited from riding on horseback, or walking on the right. "*Shimmal* [move to the left]," Muslims chided non-Muslims when they tried. But for the most part, "the *dhimmi* status had little applicability in practice," says a professor of Ottoman studies at Tel Aviv University. From the 1850s, criminal cases were heard in secular courts, where *dhimmi* status did not apply. The inclusivity made good politics. Had the Ottoman Empire not embraced its non-Muslim majority, it would never have spread so far, so fast, or survived for so long. Exclusively Muslim empires, such as the Almohad caliphate of 1121 to 1269, stirred internal opposition, and waned as rapidly as they waxed.

The Sectarianism of Secular Nationalism

When xenophobia and tolerance swapped continents is hard to determine. Though designated the sick man of Europe in the mid-nineteenth century, the Ottoman Empire took a long time dying. When Britain, the major power of the day, and its allies attacked on multiple fronts in 1915, the Ottoman Empire was still able to launch successful counter-attacks. At Gallipoli, Gaza, Aden, and Kut, the empire's army of Turks, Arabs, Kurds, Armenians, and Circassians repeatedly blunted the advances of Britain and its Indian and antipodean colonies. Two polyglot international coalitions battled each other for four years. The conflict succeeded in financing and arming a rebellion of Bedouins under Hashemite leadership, but in Iraq Sunni and Shia Arab tribes rallied to the Ottoman cause. Instead of the anticipated lightning defeat, the Ottoman Front held for four years, significantly lengthening and exacerbating the costs of the Great War.

That said, by 1914 the empire was a shrunken entity. Christian peoples and colonial powers had peeled away its western provinces on both sides of the Mediterranean, and its last hold on the northern rim of the Black Sea. European powers divvied up the empire's North African provinces, with Italy finally wresting Libya from the Ottomans in 1911. Across the Mediterranean, Greece sloughed off its Ottoman tutelage in 1829. Montenegro followed in 1851, Romania in 1856, and Serbia and Bulgaria in 1878. In the process, nationalists expelled their Muslim populations and destroyed their mosques. Russia followed its Reconquista of Circassia with a quasi-inquisition, forcing hundreds of thousands of Muslims to convert or flee aboard "floating graveyards" — decrepit boats that often sank on their way across the Black Sea.

As damaging as the loss of Ottoman territory was the loss of its pluralist ideal. In the name of *égalité*, France abolished Algeria's millet system, but then in 1870 granted French citizenship to Algeria's native Jews but not Muslims. (Jews began naming their daughters Michelle instead of Aziza.) Inside the Ottoman Empire, Western colonial powers similarly fanned confessional rivalries by championing both the replacement of religious law with a legal code stipulating equal rights for all and preferential treatment for their co-religionists. As the power of the Occident over the Orient grew, Western pressure prompted the sultan to reorganize the millet system with the Tanzimât, a uniform code which gave all equality before the law. At the same time, European consuls claimed the right to represent and protect native Christians. Benefiting from their superior access to Western officials and education and their newfound access to the state hierarchy, the

34   empire's non-Muslims rapidly rose through the Sublime Porte's ranks. Confessional tensions soared. "Our mistake was to ask for equality," says George Hintlian, who maintains the Armenian archives in Jerusalem and lost 70 relatives in the genocide. "We had everything. The bloody missionaries had opened our eyes to convince us we had nothing."

The final blow was internal. To avoid defeat after foreign powers crushed the Ottoman army and reduced its empire to ruins, Turkish nationalists, inspired by ideologies from the West, seized control and proclaimed a republic. On March 3, 1924, the last caliph, Abdülmecid II, and his Ottoman family were stripped of their nationality and titles, and dispatched from Stambouli station aboard the Orient Express. With them went the Ottoman's multi-ethnic, multi-faith ideal.

The Young Turks, who emerged out of a secular association called the Committee for Union and Progress in the first decade of the twentieth century, were a Turkish clone of the southeastern European nationalist movements that had thrust off Ottoman inclusiveness for the course of ethno-religious supremacy. They sprung from the empire's most Westernized cities, particularly Thessaloniki, and institutions, particularly the army, which with German training had replaced the Janissaries, the old force of emancipated slaves. Mustafa Kemal, or Atatürk, the father of the Turks, as he subsequently styled himself, was the blue-eyed, fair-haired son of a Macedonian born in Thessaloniki. The two leading members of the Young Turk triumvirate, Enver Pasha and Talaat Pasha, were both of Balkan stock. Initially their ideas were a composite, mixing Robespierre's anti-imperialism with romantic nineteenth-century folk nationalism, which idealized a "great and eternal land" called Turan, whose one language—Turkish—replaced the polyglot caliphate.

Initially, many non-Muslims and children of mixed-faith marriages latched onto the new movement. Its elected parliament, constitutional caliphate, and national government committed to founding a welfare state and promised the coming of a secular egalitarian age. But with the onset of the First World War and the invasion of the Anatolian heartland that soon followed, the raw nationalism of the Young Turks pushed aside whatever liberal aspirations they at first had professed. All non-Turkish and non-Muslim suspects appeared suspect. As Russia's army advanced from the east, their Armenian and Assyrian co-religionists seemed set to become the vanguard of a Russian takeover of Anatolia. It did not help that Armenian nationalists assassinated Ottoman officials and cheered for Uncle Christian, as Russia was called.

Further west, treacherous Greeks in İzmir celebrated the allied conquest of Istanbul and Christendom's recapture of Constantinople, its lost capital of Byzantium. Russian Jewish Zionists newly arrived in Jaffa looked like foreign agents bent on sloughing off Turkish rule. Ahmed Djemal Pasha, the Ottoman governor of Syria and third member of the Young Turk triumvirate, deported 6,000 of them to Alexandria, turning their settlement, Tel Aviv, into a ghost town. As minorities turned on the empire, the demise of what had been six centuries of Turkish rule seemed only a matter of time.

Of all the Ottoman Empire's Christian subjects, the Armenians had been the most loyal and the most favored. Along with the Jews, the sultan called them his *millet-i sadika*, or

36   favored community. But as the last of the Christian minorities to break with the regime, the Armenians bore the brunt of a century of pent-up revenge. Many of the perpetrators of the twentieth century's first genocide were themselves victims of milleticide. The Bushnaks, Bosnian Turks chased out by Serb secessionists, liquidated Armenians from the villages around the Anatolian city of Bitlis. Circassian Muslims, the boat people expelled by Russian Cossacks, organized the march of non-Muslims from Anatolia, in which an estimated 500,000 people died. Mehmed Reshid, a Circassian military doctor, was the governor of Diyarbakır province who gave the order to "kill microbes." In a secular age, the protective religious umbrella of the millet was no more.

The Turkish generals salvaged Anatolia for their state, but despite the passage of a century the land still feels physically and culturally hollow without its two million Armenians. All but a tenth were killed, exiled, or abducted and forced to convert. As they were marched into the desert, locals plucked women and children for concubines and *beslame*, or servant girls. Their owners changed the girls' names, erased their identities, and transposed one religion for another. Atatürk himself adopted an Armenian, raised her as his daughter, and called her Sabiha Gökçen. Her name survives as one of Istanbul's two international airports. Bereft of their women and children, Western Armenians lost the means to propagate and were denied a future.

Like their southeastern European counterparts, the Turkish generals transformed their Ottoman inheritance from a multi-faith to a mono-faith realm.

Religion became the badge of national identity. "Under the new definition any real Turk had to be a Sunni Muslim," says Edham Eldem, a Turkish historian and descendent of Enver Pasha, the Young Turk's Minister of War.

Catholic processions were banned from the streets for the first time since the sixteenth century. In 1942, the government imposed a capital tax, the Varlık Vergisi, on non-Muslims, reminiscent of the *jizya*, a tax that non-Muslim subjects historically had to pay Muslim conquerors. Amidst the Cyprus crisis in 1955, Greeks were expelled en masse from the mainland, including many who only spoke Turkish. Turkey's population of Greeks numbered 300,000 in 1920 and fell to 3,000 by the end of the century. Istanbul's last remaining Greek school has just 50 students. The irony was that the architects of the liquidation of religious pluralism were dogmatically secular. The Kemalists banned any expression of religion in public. They abolished the caliphate, sharia courts, Sufi lodges, and closed thousands of mosques.

Turkey's founders imposed a process of forced assimilation on the non-Turkish Muslims that remained. School textbooks reproduced the notion of an empire that was great when it was purely Turk, and atrophied as alien peoples seeped into its governing apparatus. The Kurds, who comprised perhaps 20 percent of the population, were subject to one of the world's most comprehensive programs of assimilation. Kurdish was banned, and its place names and history Turkified. "I couldn't speak to my grandmother," says Nurcan Baysal, a Kurdish writer and political activist in Diyarbakır, who grew up speaking Turkish.

38   Anatolia's transformation into a Turkish land was a misreading of history. The sultans never described themselves as Turks. Most of them were born to slave girls from across the empire. Like their subjects, they were a hybrid reflecting the empire's multicultural mix. And when, with British encouragement, Atatürk abolished the caliphate in 1924, the Kurds rose up the following year under Sheikh Said, a leader of the Sufi Naqshabandi order, in a failed rebellion aimed at restoring the caliphate.

On the thirteenth floor of his modest housing estate, Orhan Osmanoğlu nurses a French handkerchief embossed with the letter "H," his sole surviving possession from his great-great-grandfather Sultan Abdülhamid II. Allowed to return with other Ottoman relatives of the caliphs in 1974, he lives a modest life far removed from his ancestors' grandeur. "The republic's greatest sin was to Turkify," says Osmanoğlu. "The problem began with the word Turk. They didn't want other nationalities. The Ottomans had no problem with the Armenians. The Young Turks are the reason for the fall of the multi-cultural state."

Millet Wars

Thrust out of their Ottoman embrace, Arabs and Jews followed Turks in filling the vacuum with a notional ethnic nationalism.

In the empire's twilight years, Istanbul was abuzz with lawyers and students from across the region, imbibing the nationalism of the Young Turks and applying it to their own kind. Like the Young Turks, they were Westernized, secular, and overwhelmingly anti-religious. They aspired to supplant the empire's religious-based hierarchies with new exclusively ethnic ones, give their religious communities a territorial base and thereby assume power. In the secret societies they formed they plotted the dissection of the empire, creating new societies from old, and crafting Zionism out of Judaism and Arab nationalism out of Islam. Before he took the name of Ben-Gurion, David Grün attended the law schools in Salonika and Istanbul where Turkish ideologues

40   were fashinoning the new nationalism. Studying with him
were Yitzhak Ben-Zvi, Israel's future second president, and
Israel Shochat, the founder of the second Zionist movement's
militia arm, Hashomer, and together they developed a young
Jewish variant of the Young Turks' program. Though charier
of dismantling the world's last major Muslim power, Arab
nationalists formed *al-Muntada al-Adabi*, or the literary
forum, with branches in Syria and Iraq.

Western powers gave them succor, wise to the advantages
of fostering dependencies in the former empire. Drawing on
the Congress of Vienna in 1814–15, which had championed
the defense of minority rights in Europe, they encouraged
indigenous populations to slough off the yoke of occupying
Turks. Britain gave sanctuary to Arab nationalists in Cairo,
and France hosted the Arab Congress in Paris in 1913. Having
conquered the Middle East in the final throes of the First World
War, the two powers began demarcating the former Ottoman
Empire along sectarian lines. Syria's French governors elevated
the Sunnis in the country's central spine running from Aleppo
to Damascus, but promoted a host of other minorities on its
fringe. Lebanon was hived off from Syria and entrusted to
Christian rule in 1920. The Alawites were assigned a state
in the mountains above Latakia, and the Druze their fiefdom
in their mountain, Jebel Druze, in the south. Britain promised
the Jews a homeland in Palestine.

The paradox is that while the Second World War exposed
the danger of unfettered nationalism and resulted in the creation
of anti-national, federal models in Europe, it precipitated the
opposite in the Middle East. The Zionist movement's transfer

of the Palestinian population was short of the Young Turks' level of violence, but, combined with the chaos of war, its outcome was a similar change in the ethnic balance. By the end of the 1948 war, around 80 percent of the Palestinian population had left the new state of Israel. The new prime minister, Ben-Gurion, herded most of the remnants into demarcated enclosures and kept them under military rule until most of their land had been appropriated and their historic towns and villages reduced to rubble. Israeli leaders denied Palestinian loss and criminalized commemoration of the 1948 Palestinian Nakba, or catastrophe, in public places. They promoted the mass ingathering of their co-religionists from across Europe and the Middle East to consolidate their majority.

Arab nationalists, too, forcibly sought to establish new nation-states, replacing the Ottoman reality of a diverse and composite empire with the monochrome ideal of "an Arab world." For the most part, they preferred to achieve unity through assimilation rather than expulsion. They rewrote the histories of non-Arabs, renamed their towns and hills, and treated non-Arabic languages as alien. History textbooks celebrated a classical golden age of Islam that only began to rust when incoming Turkish mercenaries diluted Arab armies under the ninth-century Abbasid caliph al-Mu'tasim. Iraq's Ba'ath Party launched successive campaigns of Arabization, called al-Anfal (the spoils), replacing Kurds with Shias from the south. In Libya, Muammar Gaddafi branded the Berbers "mountain Arabs" and banned their language, Tamazight.

Like the Young Turks, Arab nationalists were initially inclusive of other religions. Michel Aflaq, the secular intellectual

42   who founded the Ba'ath Party, was Christian. His call to replace
      the confessional basis of statehood with ethnic Arab kinship
      appealed to non-Muslims, particularly those entering the armed
      forces, which tradition and Islamic legal codes deemed an exclu-
      sively Sunni domain. As they rose through the military ranks,
      minorities in Syria and Iraq captured the core of the state. "The
      state for all, and religion for God," ran the slogan of the Ba'ath
      Party, which sought to restrict religion to the personal sphere.

      But that religious inclusivity faced challenges from the
      first. Aflaq had noted the overlap between religion and ethnic-
      ity. "The strength of Islam, which in the past expressed that of
      the Arabs, has been reborn and has appeared in a new form,"
      he once remarked: "Arab nationalism." The Arab response to
      the Jewish conquest of Muslim land exposed and exacerbated
      the sectarian impulse lurking behind the new nationalism.
      While they quickly withdrew their armies from the battles
      in Palestine, the new Arab states turned on their own Jewish
      communities, imposing increasingly harsh conditions until
      the Jews surrendered their citizenship and left. Seventy years
      on, much of the Arab world still bears the scars. Before 1948,
      Jews comprised a quarter of Tripoli's population, concentrated
      in the Old City's Jewish quarter. Today the neighborhood lies
      crumbling alongside the towering edifice of the Corinthia,
      Africa's largest hotel. Much like the northern reaches of Jaffa,
      neighborhoods have been flattened to make way for car parks.
      The roof of the main synagogue has collapsed, its sides are
      propped up with wooden slats, and two tablets inscribed in
      Hebrew with the Ten Commandments and two Stars of David
      wobble on its facade. "Shit, it's gone," bemoaned my guide, a

conservationist, when he failed to find the chief rabbi's house.
The makings of a gray garish villa stood in its place, the cement still wet on its walls. "We were a cosmopolitan Mediterranean city, once," he said.

The exodus of some 700,000 Jews from cities across the Arab world sounded the alarm bell for other religious minorities. "After Saturday, Sunday," Christians told each other across the region.

The Triumph of Sectarian Nationalism

As the gap between the promises and the reality of secular, nationalist regimes widened, religious movements became a refuge for the disenfranchised and disaffected. Faced with the rise of godless governments across the region, religious revivalists initially cast aside sectarian differences and made common cause. Hassan al-Banna, the founder of the Sunni revivalist movement the Muslim Brotherhood, insisted that Islam had no sectarian divides. Its Shia counterpart, the Islamic Dawa Party, adopted the brotherhood's ideology and methodology wholesale. Its spiritual mentor, Muhammad Baqir al-Sadr, hailed *Social Justice in Islam*, by Muslim Brotherhood leader Sayyid Qutb, as the greatest interpretation of the Quran. His students took Qutb's *Milestones on the Road* as their manual for jihad. Sunni and Shia Islamists even joined each other's movements. One of the Dawa Party's two chapters in Basra was Sunni-led,

and in the 1950s, the Iraqi chapter of the brotherhood included
Shia members.

Then, near the close of the 1970s, regime change and
reformation in Pakistan, Iran, and Saudi Arabia gave fresh
impetus for a religious response to the failures of the first
generation of post-independence rule.

To legitimize his army takeover of Pakistan in 1978, General
Muhammad Zia-ul-Haq, a womanizer and unapologetic
consumer of alcohol, set his secular country on the path of
sharia rule. Pakistan's founders had been avowedly secular,
bent on removing not only Hindu numerical superiority but
the domination of a Sunni religious elite they regarded as a
stultifying impediment to modernization. Muhammad Ali
Jinnah, Pakistan's first leader, was Ismaili, a splinter group of
Shiism. But in his first speech as president, Zia dispensed with
such inclusivity and declared that an Islamic system was an
essential prerequisite for the country. In 1979 he replaced the
Pakistan Penal Code with the Hudood Ordinances. The laws
called for the amputation of the right hand as punishment for
robbery. Zia established "Islamic benches" in high courts to
ensure judgments complied with Islamic law, and integrated
members of Jamaat-e-Islami, the Pakistani parallel of the
Muslim Brotherhood, into Zia's bureaucracy. Pakistanis
applying for ID cards had to declare the country's Ahmadis to be
unbelievers, a requirement that is still in force.

The revolution that toppled the shah of Iran a year later
initially fired the imagination of the region's downtrodden,
Sunni and Shia alike, and threatened to trigger regime change
across the Arab world. Even the Muslim Brotherhood initially

46   embraced it. In the new spirit of ecumenism, Article 11 of the 1979 constitution appealed to all Muslims to seek political, economic, and cultural unity. But Article 5 exposed a Shia particularism that alienated Sunnis. The leader of the revolutionary state should be a Shia cleric, it declared, thereby demoting Sunni scholars to underlings.

Secular Arab leaders seized on the revolution's sectarian turn to highlight their Sunni credentials. Though the founder of the Iraqi branch of the Ba'ath Party was a Shia, it was increasingly dominated by Sunni Arabs, a minority comprising perhaps 20 percent of Iraq's population. Its leader, Saddam Hussein, stripped hundreds of thousands of Shias of their nationality, on the grounds of their Persian origin, precipitating an exodus of some five million people, including much of the country's mercantile elite. Celebration of Shia festivals and pilgrimage from Iran to Iraq's Shia holy sites was sharply curtailed. By the 1980s, religion and nationalism had been conflated not only in Israel, but across the Middle East.

For 12 centuries after the Prophet Muhammad's tribal wars, the empty quarters of the Arabian Peninsula had remained as peripheral to the course of the region's history as the Sahara. But the geographical accident of oil, and the money and foreign allies that it won, turned the peninsula into a key catalyst of Islamic political change.

Both in Ottoman times and their aftermath, the fiercely independent tribes of the Arabian Peninsula had resisted efforts to subjugate them. In the eighteenth century, the Al Saud tribe allied with an order of warrior monks founded by a local scholar,

Muhammad ibn Abd al-Wahhab. They called themselves Ahl al-
Tawhid (the people of monotheism), though others knew them
eponymously as Wahhabis.

From their base in Nejd in central Arabia, they launched
tribal raids on Shias in neighboring Iraq and the Eastern
Province, and rival Sunni tribes in Kuwait and the Hijaz. In
1926, they wrested control of Islam's holiest places, Mecca and
Medina, and assumed the old Ottoman title of Custodians of
the Holy Places. They proclaimed themselves kings, stopping
short of assuming the caliphate, on the grounds that they were
not of the Quraish, the Prophet Muhammad's tribe.

In both ideology and tactics, they were the progenitors of
contemporary jihadis. They denounced their opponents as
kaffirs, or unbelievers, who were thereby subject to the sword.
On the basis of largely dormant thirteenth-century texts, they
hounded Shias and Sunni traditionalists who venerated the
Prophet's family as practitioners of *shirk*, or polytheism. In
the name of deleting the accretions of tradition and purify-
ing the faith, they flattened shrines and demolished the old
cities of Mecca and Medina, including buildings 1,300 years
old. They leveled the Prophet's home in Medina, the seven
mosques built by his daughter, Fatimah, and the mosques of
the first caliphs in Mecca.

After their initial display of zeal, however, Saudi Arabia's
founder, King Abdulaziz, reined in the zealots, or Ikhwan.
Hundreds were slaughtered in 1930, and life on the coast regained
much of its old tempo. Cinemas in the port city of Jeddah
continued to play to packed houses and newspapers advertised
parties in the casinos and clubs on New Year's Eve. In 1979, the

48   Ikhwan—possibly sparked by the revolution in Iran—struck back. Under the leadership of Juhayman al-Otaybi, they seized control of the Grand Mosque of Mecca on the Islamic New Year of the year 1400. French commandos were finally summoned to flush them out and al-Otaybi was promptly executed, but though he lost the battle he won the war. Like-minded militants were directed with handsome support to fight communists in Afghanistan, and to bolster their internal legitimacy, the Al Sauds gave full rein to the country's conservatives to police social conduct. Application of sharia was sharply tightened, sectarian polemic intensified, and acts deemed to be an innovation at odds with the Prophet's conduct were proscribed in accordance with the teachings of Ibn Abd al-Wahhab.

Their creed enjoining the scraping away of tradition proved a property developer's dream. They built skyscrapers, like the Abraj al-Bait Towers, on the demolished Ottoman-era Ajyad Fortress, and erected garish Las Vegas-style hotels that loomed over the Kaaba, the black cube of Mecca. The house of Khadija, the Prophet's first wife, was replaced with public toilets, and the house of the first Sunni caliph, Abu Bakr, became a Hilton hotel.

The impact of the three revivalist movements on the region's geopolitics was profound. Petrodollars turned Wahhabism into the world's best-financed Islamic movement. Over the century that followed, they exported their fighters and preachers to Afghanistan and beyond. Other armed groups seeking support latched onto them, establishing satellites in isolated mountain caves in Algeria and Libya. Islam's version of the Knights Templar increasingly seemed to offer dynamism and notch successes (including the defeat of the Soviet superpower in

Afghanistan) beyond the muster of moribund Arab regimes. Bankrolled by Nejdi financiers, the transnational networks of sect and clans became the primary sources of solidarity.

The gutting of the state apparatus that followed first America's overthrow of Saddam Hussein and then of much of Syria following the uprisings of the Arab Spring cleared the ground for the Wahhabi expansion out of Saudi Arabia across the Sunni parts of the Fertile Crescent. The Middle East's compartmentalization into homogeneous units that began with the collapse of the Ottoman Empire found fresh territory to dismember. Much as in Yugoslavia, another corner of the former empire, the post-Ottoman order fractured into its rival religious parts. Out went the totalitarian nation-state; in came a centrifugal patchwork of bickering one-confessional millet states. As in the creation of Turkey and Israel, minorities left behind posed a question or problem best answered by their removal. The transformation of the non-territorial millet into the territorially demarcated millet-state precipitated mass population exchanges, torpedoing what remained of the region's pluralist past.

From world religions with universal values, the region's creeds contracted into local cults clinging to parcels of land. The history of the past century is in many ways a history of ever contracting horizons, ever more fortified border controls, and ever tighter permit regimes, as governments bent on exclusive control erect their defenses around the territorial patches in which they constitute the majority or have absolute power. While Europe dissolved its borders, the Middle East crisscrossed its once open expanse with ever more insurmountable barriers.

Creating a
Jewish State

Part Two

"Come Back, Sons"

From his vantage point on the upper reaches of Safed in the Galilee's highlands, Israel's youngest mayor, Ilan Shohat, looks out from his municipal balcony like a king surveying his realm. He points at a pedestal in the square below him, to the romantically named Davidka, or little David. It is the original mortar that in 1948 fired its projectiles in an all too general direction. On May 9, 1948, it struck an arms dump that Palestinian irregulars had stashed in the fortress on the brow of the hill, triggering an explosion so terrible that, he says, the city's Palestinian population "miraculously" fled. Zionist fighters rolled barrel bombs down the slopes into the marketplace, no doubt providing a further incentive. Centuries of existence as a shared Jewish-Muslim town ended in days.

Ever since, Safed's mayors busied themselves filling the empty space the city's Palestinians left behind. They revamped

52   the Muslim quarter, itself a misleading designation since it has
spread over not one but three quarters of the city. In its place,
they constructed an artists quarter, a Kabbalist quarter, and a
bohemian quarter. They turned the main mosque into an art
gallery, the General Exhibition, and painted dancing Hasidic
Jews in soft pastels on street maps to give the town the feel
of a Torah city. They worked with a local youth group, Banim
le-banim (building for the sons) to bring Jews the world over on
educational and volunteer programs to rebuild homes destroyed
in the 1948 war. Amplifying the call, a new yeshiva took the
name Shuvu Banim (come back, sons).

But the Muslim quarter still has the emptiness of a ghost
town. The muezzins keep their silence. Almost apologetically,
the Friday night Sabbath service in the Saraya, the former
Ottoman government compound, takes place in the basement
and not in the main hall. Someone has erected a cheap-looking
memorial to Israel's fallen in the 1948 war in the *mihrab*, or
niche, of a grand Mamluk mausoleum. Neighbors have dumped
coils of barbed wire, a rotten mattress and assorted rubbish
up the side of its *ablaq*—alternative rows of black basalt and
white limestone, though its crest of sculptured stone stalactites
hanging down from the roof still give it a look of splendor. The
defunct Great Red Mosque next door still evokes the time when
Safed was a major staging post on the road from Damascus to
the Mediterranean, not the peripheral dead-end of heavily
fortified northeastern Israel.

Shohat's attempts to revive his city as a regional hub have
met with mixed success. The bohemians who came in the 1950s
have largely left. The busloads of Jewish tourists in search of a

religious experience invest in little more than a falafel before
heading downhill to the Sea of Galilee. Universal has opened a
biscuit factory, but it has struggled to get the ultra-Orthodox out
of their yeshivas, off welfare, and onto the factory floor. Almost
as an afterthought, Shohat turned to the Arab towns surrounding Safed to support his drive for relevance the city lost in 1948.

The results have been transformative. Over the past four
years two colleges and a medical school have opened in the city,
predominantly catering to the Galilee's Arab majority. A city that
was empty of Arabs for 60 years has reconnected with its environs and its past. The high streets bustle with thousands of Arab
students. The mayor who deemed the Arab exodus a miracle now
weighs the economic and security benefits of reintegration. "If
Arabs are part of the festivities, they won't blow them up," he
says. He invited Palestinian president Mahmoud Abbas, a refugee from Safed, to visit ("though not to stay"). And he has even
helped open the first cracks in the barriers that for three decades
have barred contact between Israel and Syria. Over the course
of Syria's civil war, Safed's Ziv Medical Center has treated hundreds of Syrian victims, who are often accompanied by their
relatives. They might yet serve as ambassadors for a future co-
existence, Shohat says. The possibilities seem endless.

The backlash was not long in coming. Ultra-Orthodox Jews
leave messages on his answering machine protesting that
Arab students renting in the depressed housing estates
they share desecrate the Sabbath by playing loud music
and smoking water pipes. To appease the outcry, he went on
campus appealing to Arab students to help with the Passover

54   spring clean by whitewashing ultra-Orthodox homes. He also launched a festival of oriental music for Sephardi Jews and local Arabs hoping they might play together. But the accusations that he has opened the gates for Arab as well as Jewish sons to return keep growing. God forbid, soon the students will want to reopen the Great Red Mosque for Friday prayers, protests a burly blond-haired yeshiva student in the white woolly cap of the Na Nach, a popularized form of the Breslov Hasidic order. "Never again."

The town's chief rabbi, a salaried government appointee, led several dozen rabbis in issuing a *psak din*, the Jewish equivalent of a fatwa, banning Jews from selling or renting homes to Arabs. "Jews should not flee from Arabs, they should make the Arabs flee," admonished Safed's chief rabbi, Shmuel Eliyahu. To publicize it he organized a town hall meeting under the banner "The Quiet War — Fighting Decay in the Holy City of Safed." Developers moved in, building plush Jewish-only estates offering "Jewish air." Far from taking action against his state employees, in 2013 Prime Minister Benjamin Netanyahu appointed one of the *psak din*'s signatories, Rabbi Shai Piron, his education minister.

Over 400 Palestinian villages were erased in or after the 1948 war, but Palestine's urbanscape suffered more than its landscape. Before the exodus, a third of the Palestinian population lived in cities. Many a family built an architectural gem. Palestinian cinemas, theatre halls, and printing houses abounded. By the end of 1948, 90 percent stood vacant. Palestine's cosmopolitan, educated middle class was broken.

Four generations on, it is finally beginning to revive. In part because their own villages and towns are hemmed within tight planning zones and overcrowded, Palestinians have begun to repopulate the coastal cities once again. Students attending universities on the coast put down roots. In a few places Jewish and Arab graduates have created bohemian neighborhoods that consciously seek to lay the foundations for a post-conflict society and attempt to replace the traditional hierarchies of Jewish owners and Arab laborers with a non-sectarian bourgeoisie. "We are not only serving, we are ordering," says a bartender in an Arab-owned bar on Masada Street in the port city of Haifa, in one of Israel's first neighborhoods where the ownership, workforce, and clientele of local amenities and cafés are mixed. Isha-l-Isha (woman to woman), Israel's oldest grassroots feminist association, has an Arab chairwoman and insists on a joint Jewish-Arab administration and staff. Some see the seeds of a more egalitarian future. "When I was my 17-yearold daughter's age, I didn't dare speak Arabic in public," says a Haifa lawyer. "It was like handing yourself in. Now we do it everywhere."

Mayors of municipalities with mixed Arab and Jewish populations have long oscillated between serving as ciphers of and cushions against nationalist politicians at the center. Many are torn between espousing a multi-cultural, cosmopolitan city and a Jewish one that Zionism promised to build, and even the most liberal flinch from describing their cities as shared. Most opt instead for an ad hoc approach that might be described as *ad kan*, Hebrew for just so much, preserving the dominant status of Hebrew and Jewish culture. While Tel Aviv celebrated its first centenary with a dazzling show of white lights, the mayor of Haifa, Yona Yahav, shied from marking his city's 250th anniversary lest it revive memories of its Palestinian past.

Yahav is a web of contradictions. He fought in Israel's formative wars and then climbed the ranks of the Labor Party when it was the prime driver of Zionism. He opposed the construction of new Arabic schools, churches, or mosques in districts that were once Jewish but are now distinctly mixed. And yet he has gone further than other mayors in ensuring his own staff is mixed. Israeli Palestinians head its finance and, perhaps more significantly, conservation departments. He has flouted demands from Netanyahu's transport minister to Hebraize Israel's streets name, naming a roundabout after Emil Habibi, a leading local Palestinian writer and politician. He let an Arabic hip-hop band, Ministry of Dub-Key, perform in front of the Haifa Museum of Art. And he broke a tacit ban on celebration of non-Jewish festivals in public, staging a "Festival of Festivals," marking Christmas while discreetly avoiding its name. Initially, the municipality balked at erecting a Christmas tree, but in 2010 it installed a plastic-bottle tree, and two years later a real tree with a small menorah alongside it, lest anyone forget it was Hanukkah.

Governments in other historically Arab cities are also tentatively opening a door to the past. In 2009 Lod began hosting a joint Arabic and Hebrew music festival, and in 2011 opened its first state high school for Arabs. The desk of Lod's deputy mayor, Aviv Wasserman, is covered with designs for his "megaplan"—the reconstruction of the old medina *souq* that army bulldozers largely leveled after the 1948 war. Though as

yet merely an architect's fancy on paper, the project provides
for renovation of the dilapidated buildings that survived the
wreckage. "We want to restore it to how it looked in 1948," says
Wasserman. After years of resisting calls to erect a signpost
listing Acre's name in Arabic at the city's entrance, the
municipality agreed.

And yet every year or two, just when the country seems to
be normalizing, national politics intervenes and Israel has
another battle with its neighbors, which refreshes nationalist
animosities. Though the 2014 Gaza War was in Israel's far south
and Safed was out of reach of its rockets, Shohat dismissed
any Arab municipal worker suspected of sympathizing with
Gaza on social media, and advised Arab students to go back to
their villages on security grounds. Jewish militants in the city
relaunched their campaign, scrawling "Death to Arabs" on Arab
front doors, to make the city Arab-free once again.

While the world's headlines focused on Israel's bombardment of Gaza, the battle inside Israel went largely unreported.
In response to the killing of three Jewish students outside their
Torah college in a West Bank settlement, Israel's government
fanned calls for reprisals. "Vengeance for the blood of three
pure youths," Netanyahu posted on his Twitter account, calling their killers "human animals." Israeli television suspended
normal scheduling, and broadcast rolling coverage of their
funerals, while a mob a few hundred strong spilled onto central
Jerusalem's Jaffa Road, crying death to Arabs. The manager of
a shoe shop stood his ground at the shop door to deny entry
to thugs baying for his Palestinian assistants, but a guard at

58   McDonald's proved less effective. For three hours, the mob ran amok. Policemen who tried to restrain them were mocked as Arab-lovers. Some boarded trams and tried to lynch Palestinian passengers. Before dawn the next morning, Jews abducted a Palestinian boy, doused him in gasoline, and burned him to death in a Jerusalem forest. The police delayed release of the autopsy, and spread rumors that it was an inside job. "It might have been a relative pursuing an honor crime for homosexuality," said Micky Rosenfeld, Israel's police spokesman and a settler from Britain. No Israeli channel stopped normal transmission for the boy's funeral.

Fired with emotion, Israel went to war in Gaza, further exacerbating communal tensions within. "We won't let them destroy Haifa's co-existence and harmony," Yona Yahav told me, denouncing Palestinians who staged an anti-war protest in his city. Radio Haifa broadcast a call for a Jewish counter-rally, and on his way to the first demonstration the city's Arab deputy mayor, Suhail Assad, and his son were mugged. As sirens rang out their alarms across Israel's cities warning of incoming rockets, Israel's foreign minister, Avigdor Lieberman, urged Jews to boycott Arab shops and restaurants. Palestinians closed ranks. "We're telling Israel that our Palestinian identity is more important to us than our Israeli citizenship," Jamal Zahalka, an Israeli Arab parliamentarian, who galvanized protesters. Armed riot police moved into Arab towns, dispersing protesters with tear gas and stun grenades. Stone-throwers struck back, forcing the closure of Israel's main north-south artery, Road 6. Communal interaction all but collapsed. Parents and children from Jerusalem's only mixed school of Arabs and Jews, Hand in

Hand, walked twice a week through the city just chatting to show it was still possible. They were heckled as they went. Arsonists spray-painted "Cancer" on its walls and set a classroom on fire. Palestinians stopped going into West Jerusalem, especially by tram, in part out of fear, in part as a boycott. Sales at Jewish-run malls, which normally soared during Ramadan, slumped. Even after the police sprayed skunk into the shops of East Jerusalem's main shopping street, Saladin, and the smell hung for days in the air, Palestinians continued shopping in their own neighborhoods.

"Redeeming the Land"

For Israel's Palestinians, the 2014 Gaza war highlighted their powerlessness. While Israeli Jews cheered the televised footage of Gaza's bombardment, Palestinians watched in horror as their relatives, turned into refugees in 1948, faced the offensive alone. Israel's rules of engagement determined that anyone remaining in a district after advance warning of a bombardment was an enemy combatant, not a civilian, but Israel and Egypt had both sealed Gaza's gates, closing their paths for escape.

Though comprising 20 percent of the population, Israel's Arabs had long been conditioned to accept their exclusion from the country's decision-making, but just asking questions now raised the possibility of arrest or dismissal from work. On paper, Israel's declaration of independence in May 1948 promised equality and full citizenship to Jews and non-Jews alike. But in the nation-state of the Jews, as Netanyahu's government called

Israel, they no longer belonged. Although Arabs had the vote, in
70 years Israel's leaders had never included their parties in government, or appointed an Arab to run a ministry. The Nakba was
not a finite event after which life returned to normal—it was a
continuum.

If the government had been out of sync with its people there
might have been some relief. But since 2009, a large majority of
Israeli Jews had voted the right-wing into power. In polls, 47 percent of Israeli Jews favored expelling Israel's Arab citizens to
the West Bank or Gaza, 42 percent expressed an aversion to living in the same bloc as Arabs, and a third believed Arabs should
be denied a vote. Many Jews accepted the social conditioning
unquestioningly. From birth, segregation is not only sanctioned
but institutionalized. Education up to university level remains
almost entirely segregated

The army only reinforces the divisions. "To defeat our
enemies, and that is the goal of the army, we need less pluralism
and more Jewish awareness," said Brigadier General Avichai
Rontzki, then the army's chief rabbi. Hosting a highly publicized
Bible study in his home, Netanyahu—a secular Jew whose Jewish
observance is more a public than a private affair (he rejects the
Jewish dietary code and once married a non-Jew)—extolled the
Book of Joshua, a story of the Jewish conquest of the land, as
a template for dealing with contemporary difficulties. "From
Joshua we mainly draw the understanding that our enemies
must be fought," he told his audience.

For most of its history, Israelis left the task of fighting
Palestinians to their security forces. Communal clashes were
remarkably rare. But with the intervals between Israel's cycle

62   of offensives on Palestinians shortening, the military mindset
that dominates during war and mobilizes civilians as well as
soldiers to the effort has scant time to subside.

If economic growth had been his first concern, Shimon Gafsou,
the mayor of Nazareth Illit, might have welcomed the influx
of thousands of middle-class Palestinians from cramped Arab
Nazareth up the hill to his shrinking city.

Instead he worked to keep them out. He barred the opening
of churches, mosques, or Arab schools, and rather than provide
for the education of the city's 1,900 Arab children, he opened
a yeshiva instead. "Jews, Jews, Jews," proclaimed his campaign
posters in the 2013 local election. "Upper Nazareth will be
Jewish forever."

The city's three public libraries stocked Hebrew, English,
Russian, French, and Spanish books, but not Arabic ones. "No
more shutting our eyes, no more relying on the law that lets
every citizen live where he wants," he told me. "This is the time
to defend our home." When Arab residents protested the discrimination, Gafsou, a secular politician, cited God's injunction
to Moses in Numbers 33:55:

But if ye will not drive out the inhabitants of the land from
before you; then it shall come to pass, that those which ye
let remain shall be pricks in your eyes, and thorns in your
sides, and shall vex you in the land wherein ye dwell.

"Mayors rightly don't want mixed cities," said Ariel Atias,
Israel's housing minister from 2009 to 2013, by way of support.
"It's unsuitable [for Jews and Arabs] to live together."

But when the reverse happened and Jews moved into prime real estate inhabited by Arabs, he offered fulsome backing. With government funding, rabbis descended from settlements in the West Bank highlands and opened new Torah schools and sponsored *garinim*, or seed communities, in Arab neighborhoods on the coastal plain. Rabbis recited martial verses from the Bible and presented them as a manual for contemporary conduct, with rousing sermons about "the Jewish fighting spirit" evident in David's slaying of Goliath. In the wake of their failure to prevent the closure of Israel's settler enterprise in Gaza, they were anxious, too, to establish footholds in Israel proper and regain popular support. Applying the same narrative they used to win public support for the settlements, they called for "redeeming the land." If 500 settlers, with help from Israel's army, could occupy the heart of Hebron, a city of 300,000 Palestinians, they could do the same, they reasoned, amongst concentrations of Arabs in the old Palestinian cities of Jaffa, Acre, Lod, and Ramla, which from the eighth to the eleventh century had been Palestine's capital.

Between Netanyahu's second election victory in 2009 and his fourth in 2015, 38 churches and mosques were attacked, burned, or defaced in a campaign its perpetrators termed price-tag. Not a single vandal was charged. Hard-line rabbis warned with impunity of the threat Arab male libidos posed to Jewish women, and their followers spread their messages on social media, and inner-city lampposts coated with luminous stickers. "Arab, don't even dare to think about Jewish girls," read one.

Lehava, an Israeli NGO that took its name from the Hebrew acronym for "preventing assimilation in the holy land," published a "Page of Disgrace," shaming "unfaithful women

64 who, out of choice and ideology, chose to leave the Jewish people and openly live with *goyim*." Their calling cards read: "If you are in contact with a *goy*, or you know a girl who is, get in touch." They rallied their 35,000 Facebook followers to disrupt inter-faith wedding parties, and at night, donned black T-shirts with a yellow Star of David, and went looking for Arab couples to accost in West Jerusalem's backstreets. One summer evening in the midst of the 2014 Gaza war, a teenage girl caught me watching as she kicked a car with an Arab couple in it, and spat in my face. "*Dai*, enough," cried a passerby in a loose white cotton dress, and collapsed in tears at the scene. "Hug me, please."

Debates in parliament and national television reports about Lehava's operations to "rescue," rather than abduct, Jewish women who married Arab men lent their narrative an air of respectability. The Committee on the Status of Women and Gender Equality held a debate on the dangers of inter-marriage to mark "Jewish Identity Day" in the Knesset.

The Politics of Memory

A Palestinian refugee returning to his homeland after 70 years would feel he was entering a foreign land. The ancient stepped terraces of the hillsides have been hidden beneath pine woods, turning a Levantine scene into an Alpine one. Of the 500 mosques the state sequestrated after 1948, some survive as prisons or pubs, while the others are boarded up. Muslim cemeteries have been paved over and turned into roads. Israel's religious affairs ministry lists only Jewish places of worship as holy sites.

Immediately after the 1967 war, bulldozers flattened the twelfth-century Moroccan neighborhood that Saladin built to create a vast plaza for prayer in front of the Western Wall of what was once Jerusalem's biblical temple.

The antiquities department determines which sites holy to other faiths are worthy of preservation, but has not stopped the destruction. In 2012, a zealot eluded the copious cameras

66   placed around the Old City and took a hammer to the turquoise
      Ottoman tiles that since the seventeenth century had graced
      King David's Tomb on Mount Zion up the hill. Insisting the
      damage was beyond repair, the authorities then finished the
      job, removing the fragments to expose Jerusalem stone beneath
      and turn what had been a Christian and Muslim shrine into a
      synagogue. "We cleaned it," the tomb's curator told me. The
      police abandoned the hunt for the perpetrator.

      The Nea Ekklesia of Theotokos, a sixth-century Byzantine
      church whose grandeur once rivaled Constantinople's Hagia
      Sophia, is also slipping out of view. Situated in the heart of the
      Jewish quarter, a part of Jerusalem's occupied Old City Israel has
      designated for Jewish development, the authorities consider
      it out of keeping with their narrative of exclusive Jewish
      possession. A car park covers its exposed nave, and access to
      the chapel runs through a children's kindergarten and a series
      of locked gates. The East Jerusalem Development Foundation, a
      government-appointed body overseeing the Old City's services,
      has a key, but requests go largely unanswered. Like other church
      ruins in the Jewish quarter, there are no tourist signs to point to
      its whereabouts.

      Each year on Jerusalem Day, right-wing Zionists celebrate
      Israel's capture of the Old City in 1967 by marching through
      the Muslim quarter, as if rehearsing a takeover. Their youth
      groups commandeer school buses and ferry their throng to its
      gates. "For their own safety," the police order Muslim residents
      indoors and barricade off the side streets.

      At sundown, national-religious Jews reenact Pamplona's
      Running of the Bulls—without the bulls. In the hours before

the charge, Palestinian shopkeepers remove the fluorescent bulbs from over their thresholds, padlock their shutters, and vanish. The hawkers and women selling vine leaves squatting on the steps of the grand Ottoman portal of Damascus Gate pack up their wares and withdraw. "There are no Arabs," exclaimed a delighted Orthodox Jewish American tourist as she arrived to watch tens of thousands of religious Zionist stream down the hill from West Jerusalem through Damascus Gate. "Arabs go home," they chanted as they entered the Muslim quarter's al-Wad Street, and banged their fists on their metal shutters. Many wore armbands declaring "Kahane was right," honoring the Israeli parliamentarian and rabbi who championed the expulsion of Arabs. "No one will stop us from rebuilding blessed Jerusalem," cries Shmuel Rabinowitz, the rabbi of the Western Wall, welcoming the crowds as they converge on his plaza. For one night all the Old City's quarters are Jewish.

If Jerusalem's Old City is the focal point of religious Zionist ambitions, the Dome of the Rock, where Judaism's biblical shrine had once stood, is its apex. For Muslims, its esplanade and the Al Aqsa mosque alongside are the third holiest place of pilgrimage, where Muhammad ascended to heaven. Three million Muslims pray there annually, compared to some 400,000 Christian visitors and 10,000 Jews.

Traditionally, the site is subject to a rabbinic ban, violation of which incurs a premature death. Only Jews ritually purified with the ashes of a red heifer, said the rabbis, could enter Judaism's most sacred ground, a task needing divine intervention, since the red heifer is widely considered extinct.

68   But in recent decades, some national-religious activists have argued that God needs a helping hand. The construction of the Third Temple, the coronation of a messiah, and the application of the Jewish law, *halaka*, they reasoned, are all human deliverables. Once realized, they would usher in the true Torah State in place of one they deem secular, corrupt and compromising.

Right-wing parliamentarians in the Knesset offered a helping hand. They promoted legislation to give them a foothold on the Temple Mount, allocating a Jewish space where they could pray. When they lost the vote, they beseeched the police force to restrict Muslim access and expand that of Jews'. In the summer of 2014, the police obliged. Palestinians under 55 were barred access, and those over 55 had to leave their ID cards with police before entering the esplanade.

Introduced on Laylat al-Qadr (the Islamic night of decree), when the Quran was first revealed to Muhammad and Islam's holiest night, and in the midst of the 2014 Gaza war, the new restrictions could not have been better timed to inflame. The previous year hundreds of thousands of families had thronged to the esplanade, spending the night camped out on its ancient paving stones. Now it was all but empty. Youths calling themselves the Mourabitoun, or religious sentinels, who had entered the Temple Mount before the ban came into effect, set the Israeli security post at the entrance to al-Aqsa alight.

Zionist rabbis also rallied their flock to the mount. Moshe Feiglin, the Knesset's then deputy speaker and a senior parliamentarian in Netanyahu's Likud Party, arrived with an armed escort. In partial deference to the rabbinic injunction against violating hallowed ground, he took off his shoes and ascended the steps of the Dome of the Rock, where the temple's inner sanctuary had stood. "Remove all Muslims from the Temple Mount," he harangued the police.

Inside al-Aqsa Mosque, the Mourabitoun upturned bookcases and used them as barricades. They hid behind and aimed firecrackers at riot police. Police shot back with stun grenades and tear gas. At 11 a.m., when Jewish visiting hours were complete, Israel's forces withdrew, leaving the mosque floor strewn with cartridges. Youths caked in powered limestone to dampen the effects of the tear gas emerged undefeated and immediately began hurling stones at the riot police from the esplanade's gates. The police shot back, and elderly worshippers and this writer took cover behind the mosque's marble pillars retching from the tear gas. Had the carpets caught fire, al-Aqsa's mufti told me, the mosque might have gone up in flames. The Muslim world—Shias and Sunnis as one—would have set aside their sectarian differences and rushed in, perhaps deposing the Jordanian king en route. That evening, halfway down its bulletin, Israel's media reported another day of Muslim rioting on the Temple Mount.

The Israeli government justifies its recourse to force on the basis that anything short of a heavy hand might be mistaken for weakness. But the demand for recognition of its Jewish claims, while denying those of others, can trouble even its sympathizers.

Of all Jerusalem's established sects, the Armenians were the weakest. In 2009, they erected a monument to their victims of the 1915 genocide anticipating empathy from a population

70   deeply enveloped in its own experience of genocide. Instead
      the authorities ignored the Armenian patriarch's appeals and
      banned its public display. Each day tens of thousands pass by an
      unremarkable green iron fence on the road from the Old City's
      Jaffa Gate to the Jewish quarter unaware of the monument lying
      behind. At first, the patriarch thought that Israel feared for
      its relations with Turkey. When Turkish-Israeli relations
      approached a breaking point, he wondered whether the crosses
      on the monument caused offense. Then the municipality
      suggested a slice of church land might sway the mayor.
      Ultimately, it seemed, Israel feared the monument might
      threaten its assertion of the uniqueness of its genocide.

      Each year, Israel's Holocaust Day—it marks a different one
      from the rest of the world—begins with Ashkenazi cantors
      reciting the official dirges for the dead in Israel's state memo-
      rial, Yad Vashem, and ends in the far north of the country, at the
      Ghetto Fighters' House, with a military tribute in which Israel's
      top general vows the Holocaust will never happen again. A fresh
      corps of Israeli army cadets descends the steps of an open-air
      amphitheater bearing flaming torches. Addressing the nation
      Netanyahu reminded his people in 2014 that Israel was "stron-
      ger than ever" and "pulsates with an iron will to ensure the
      future of our people." After the generals, politicians and mili-
      tary troupes had marched off, a diminutive, frail Holocaust
      86-year-old survivor walked onto the vast stage, and spoke in a
      still small voice.

      "We have secured our physical existence, not our values,"
      said Haviva Aranyi. "They are in danger." The Holocaust, she
      said, began not with the election of Adolf Hitler, but the decades

of hate speech and social exclusion that preceded it. The following morning, over a breakfast of sliced cucumbers in her bungalow on a kibbutz near the border with Lebanon, she was still elated from the reception her had received (the audience had clapped for her speech alone), but described her unease at the country she had lived in for 60 years. She fretted that Israel was hemorrhaging its humanism by incarcerating Palestinians in walled enclaves. "We have to keep asking how genocide happened, to stop it happening again," said Aranyi, who as a Hungarian partisan had broken the locks of rail carriages carrying Jews to concentration camps. "Elsewhere. And here." Each year some 100,000 soldiers pass through the halls of the Yad Vashem, carrying their guns. On the news, Netanyahu rehearses his scare-mongering polemic that each generation produces a new exterminator of the Jews, and the military is the guarantor of the Jewish nation's survival. At the entrance to his refurbished office on the border with Gaza, Israel's Southern Division Commander has hung two photos, one "Warsaw ghetto boy" and another of a shower of phosphorus munitions exploding over Gaza City.

A host of Israeli pedagogues have appealed for a reappraisal of Israel's Holocaust syllabus, in hopes of promoting universal values of anti-racism, tolerance, and humanism over the particularist narrative of self-reliance at any cost. All people have the potential for genocide, says Yehuda Bauer, Israel's preeminent Holocaust historian, who is now in his nineties. He worries that Netanyahu's government "misuses and abuses" the Holocaust, using its message to justify interning "the external threat" of asylum seekers. Though they are fleeing genocide in southern

72   Sudan or Eritrea, whose regime has one of the world's worst
      human rights records, Netanyahu commits them to "modern
      concentration camps" in the desert, he protests. But even the
      country's liberal press seem to have tired of his diatribes, he
      complains. "We have become a nation of bystanders."

      At Israel's second, smaller Holocaust museum, the
      Ghetto Fighters' House, the curators also worry about the ris-
      ing nationalist tide, which they consider a core ingredient
      of genocide, and have opened the Center for Humanistic
      Education in the hope of offering a remedy. Its tally of Second
      World War fatalities lists the seven million German dead
      above the six million Jews. While Yad Vashem has closed down
      its program for Arab students, the center offers joint courses
      for Arab and Jewish students, often—given Israel's segregated
      education system—meeting for the first time. Rather than
      teach the Holocaust as "Jewish family history," they examine
      how racism overran Nazi Germany and scrutinize their own
      society for modern methods of social exclusion. Across a
      black wall, white letters float upward to form the names of the
      4,800 villages destroyed in the Holocaust, before separating
      and dissolving again. In the darkness the facilitator encour-
      ages the students to tell the stories of their grandparents who
      might also have lost their villages. "My grandmother fled
      Romania and rebuilt her life in Israel," one student says. "I've
      never met my grandmother," says another. "She was expelled
      in 1948 to Lebanon, aged four. We speak sometimes on Skype."

      I ask the curators whether they might display the names
      of the 450 Arab villages lost after Israel's creation alongside
      those of Jewish villages in Eastern Europe, or erect a plaque

to the Palestinian village of Samaria, on whose ruins the museum was built. They say they are strapped for funds, and worry that they could be deemed criminals under legislation banning the use of public funds to remember the Nakba, which was pushed through the Knesset by Netanyahu's government. The program already attracts three times as many Arab teenagers as Jews, and the local authorities are threatening to scrap it. "The Arabs want to engage with the past. For the Jews it is easier not to know," one of the supervisors tells me. "I don't want to feel perpetually accused," one of his Jewish students protested.

Two months after Aranyi ended the Ghetto Fighters' House commemoration, Netanyahu unleashed Israel's worst devastation of Palestine since 1948. For 50 days Gaza was a target bank. Some 2,200 people were killed, the oldest aged 92 and the youngest four days old. Extended families died in a single bombardment. Even the country's liberal newspaper, *Haaretz*, which in normal times might have held the government to account, joined the war effort. News bulletins on Channel 10, supposedly the most critical of Israel's television networks, reported the terror campaign Gaza had waged against Israel with its rockets, which as on most days inflicted no casualty, alongside coverage of buxom girls sunbathing on tanks. There was no mention of the devastation in Gaza. Banners hung from balconies enjoining Israelis to "hug a Golani," the name of an elite infantry brigade on the front line. Daniella Weiss, a popular radio presenter, silenced a rare Palestinian interviewee who spoke of scores of children

74 killed by their artillery in Shujaiyia, a Gaza suburb where he lived. "We don't know the real numbers," she insisted.

Unable to rely on the media to broadcast the Palestinian death toll, an Israeli human rights group, B'Tselem, commissioned an advertisement. The broadcasting authority banned it. Unaware of the destruction Israel had inflicted, a survey reported that 45 percent of Israeli Jews felt Netanyahu had used too little firepower on Gaza; only 6 percent thought he had used too much.

At an audience of American immigrants at a synagogue in Beit Shemesh, midway between Tel Aviv and Jerusalem, Moshe Feiglin, the Likud firebrand who walked proprietarily on the steps of the Dome of Rock, proposed killing tens of thousands of Hamas members and expelling Gaza's 1.8 million people "in accordance with humanitarian standards." Retired American doctors, army officers, and judges munched on carrot sticks and pretzels and nodded. "Just nuke 'em," said a young American woman.

In different times, Israel's Western allies might have held it in check. But preoccupied with turmoil elsewhere in the region, both they and Israel's erstwhile Arab foes were too busy on other fronts. So commonplace and large was the population displacement and sectarian cleansing elsewhere in the region that Israel's six decades of dispossession of Palestinians appeared, if not paltry, a regional norm. The 2014 Gaza offensive, its most punitive to date, taught Netanhayu that he could act with effective impunity. European powers wrung their hands, but shied from taking action.

For all its insistence on its differences, Israel was part of the club of sectarian Middle East states in which one millet

suppressed and bullied another in order to reign supreme. It
called itself a democracy but so gerrymandered the borders
and restricted access to citizenship that though it ruled
over a non-Jewish majority, Jews comprised 90 percent of its
parliamentarians.

The Resurgence of Sunnistan

Part Three

The Palestinian Origins of Sunni Milletism

Surrounded by broken headstones in an untended corner of a cemetery in Haifa lies the grave of Izz ad-Din al-Qassam. His graveyard is covered in weeds and smashed glass. Its gates are rusted and unhinged. Periodically, vandals smash his tombstone. State utility companies pursue a more organized assault. A sewage pipe flows next to his headstone. The highway that races past is slated for expansion. And in 2014, the authorities earmarked the cemetery for sale to a private construction company building a trans-Galilee railroad. Few settings could be more ignominious for the progenitor of Sunni jihadism.

Al-Qassam's victories while alive were limited. As a chaplain in the Ottoman army, he raised a 250-man volunteer force to resist Italy's colonial project in Libya, but never got further than the Levantine port of Alexandretta. He helped launch the resistance against France's occupation of Syria, but he fled over the border to

78   British-occupied Palestine after he was sentenced to death. Too
fiery for the established clerics of Jerusalem, al-Qassam was sent
to preach to stevedores at Haifa's port and tour rural Palestine as
a marriage registrar. In 1935, he declared a jihad against Britain
for bequeathing his homeland to the Jews, but a week later was
gunned down by a squad on patrol in the southern Galilee hills.

Only as a martyr did al-Qassam enjoy success. His call to
arms salved Islam's wounded pride after a century in which
Sunni Muslims had seen their reach inexorably contract in
the face of European expansion, and launched a new school of
Islamic activism. He fashioned a theology of war readily acces-
sible to the peasants and laborers he preached to and tapped the
resentment against the patricians—"a people of rabbits," as he
called them. "You must know," said al-Qassam, "that nothing
will save us but arms."

The Palestinian impetus for jihadi Islam has been under-
stated. Israel's sympathizers shy from the suggestion that they
might have spawned global jihad, and Palestine's sympathizers flinch at the suggestion that they might have had a hand in
the world's prime terrorist threat. Though they make up only
0.6 percent of the world's Muslim population, for four generations Palestinians have developed and disseminated the
ideological tenets of transnational jihadism. As the first Sunni
Arab mass diaspora in modern times, they played a key role in
fashioning and disseminating a pan-Islamic vision unfettered by
national boundaries and in forging a transnational network.

A generation after al-Qassam another Palestinian founded
al-Qaeda. Abdullah Azzam was seven years old when Israel

captured some of his father's land in the West Bank village of
Silat al-Harithiya during the 1948 Nakba. As a teen he joined
the Muslim Brotherhood and preached in villages around his
home, including Burqin, which retains a reputation as a base for
Islamic jihad. He studied at Kadoorie Institute, an agricultural
school in the quaint West Bank town of Tulkarm, established
by a Jewish philanthropist who engraved his name in Hebrew
on the threshold. He then studied sharia at the University of
Damascus in Syria, graduating with highest honors in 1966. The
next year, Israel completed the occupation of the West Bank in
the Six-Day War, forcing Azzam and his family to join a quarter
of a million refugees in the Palestinian exodus to Jordan.

From the heights of the Jordanian mountains in Ajloon
overlooking his homeland, Azzam established a training camp
for militants. "It gave him a first taste of mountain hideouts,"
recalls Abu Obeida, a Syrian Palestinian who fought with Azzam
in Jordan and later joined him as his bodyguard in Afghanistan.
In his *Memories of Palestine*, Azzam describes how, as a 28-year-
old schoolteacher of religious studies with no military training,
he led guerilla operations against Israel as well as Quranic study
circles. Much as he would later do in Afghanistan against the
Soviets, he attracted Islamists from across the Arab world,
including, briefly, Rached Ghannouchi, the future head of
Tunisia's Islamist movement, Ennahda. Azzam called the oper-
ational bases he led al-Qawa'id—plural of al-Qaeda.

In 1970, Yasser Arafat's nationalist Palestinian Liberation
Organization fought King Hussein for the control of Jordan in
the Black September civil war. Arafat lost and the Palestinian
fighters, including Azzam, were expelled. He found sanctuary

80   in Saudi Arabia as a lecturer in Islamic law at King Abdulaziz University in Jeddah. Amongst his recruits was a young engineering student named Osama bin Laden.

In the crackdown that followed the seizure by jihadis of the Grand Mosque at Mecca in 1979, Saudi Arabia dismissed Azzam from his university post and encouraged him instead to raise the flag of Jihad for Afghanistan, which the Soviets had invaded that year. With the endorsement of Saudi Arabia's grand mufti, Azzam issued a fatwa declaring a jihad on the Soviets, and headed to Pakistan to set up a training camp. To drum up political and financial support, he toured the globe, including dozens of cities in the United States. The bin Laden family and Western intelligence agencies were amongst his most avid donors, funding the training of over 16,000 warrior-students. The investment paid off. Having forced the Soviets from Kabul, he penned a vision for the reconquest of Sunni lands. The jihad should continue, he wrote shortly before his assassination in 1989, "until all other lands that were Muslim are returned to us, so that Islam will reign again." Palestine headed the list.

The eruption of the First Intifada in 1987 refocused attention on Palestine. The local branch of the Muslim Brotherhood abandoned its quietest posture and formed Hamas. Prime Minister Yitzhak Rabin deported 415 Hamas leaders bound and blindfolded into Lebanon in 1992, but the transfer only served to "transform us from a besieged parochial movement into an international one, and gave us a gateway to the world," recalls Imad al-Falouji, at the time a Hamas leader who had registered to join the Afghan jihad. Through Hezbollah,

Hamas established diplomatic, financial, and military ties with
Iranian and Syrian advisors, and created a military apparatus,
the Izz ad-Din al-Qassam Brigades. In April 1993, Hamas
conducted Sunni Islam's first suicide bombing at Mehola, in
the occupied Jordan Valley. Applying techniques acquired from
Hezbollah, it embraced Hezbollah's veneration of suffering and
martyrdom, overcoming a religious ban on suicide.

But though it bequeathed a new and increasingly favored
militant tactic, Hamas stepped back from acquiring a regional
role. It strictly limited its operations to Palestine, and acted
against activists that favored broadening the jihad. With Azzam
dead, bin Laden in increasingly muzzled hiding, and Hamas
rigidly limiting their theater of operations, the task of rousing
the struggle for Sunni reconquest fell to a third generation of
Palestinian ideologues.

Abu Qatada al-Filistini and Abu Muhammad al-Maqdisi make
an unlikely duo. The former is big and burly, the latter scrawny.
Side by side they look a bit like Laurel and Hardy. Al-Maqdisi
dresses immaculately in a lean and ironed black *galabia* with
two pens in his chest pocket and a pointed reddish brown beard,
which he might have hennaed. When Abu Qatada sits down,
by contrast, he splays his ogre's limbs. His beard is scraggy,
unkempt, and salt-and-peppered.

Their friendship had matured over shared times in
Kuwait and Afghanistan, where as Arab volunteers they had
battled the Russians in the late 1980s. When I met them in
Abu Qatada's home in a northern suburb of Amman, Jordan,
in November 2014, they had both emerged from long spells

in prison and were delighted to discover the black ensign of jihad flying across much of the region. From the comfort of their living-room couches, both savored its expansion on the news bulletins. Abu Qatada's home was ornate. His salon was adorned with white lilies and a bowl of pink-painted cones on a low coffee table. In their absence jihad had made many technological advances. Abu Qatada pawed his cat fondly and giggled at an Instagram picture on al-Maqdisi's phone of a kitten dressed in an explosive suicide belt. His young son had chosen a mobile ringtone of the crash of an incoming missile followed by a jihadi dirge. "I'm labeled the world's fifth most dangerous terrorist," al-Maqdisi smirks proudly, scanning an anti-jihadist website.

Together they pored over map a of Palestine. Abu Qatada pointed to Beit Sahour, the West Bank town where he was born in 1959 and where shepherds had watched their flocks on the slopes of Bethlehem two millennia earlier. Al-Maqdisi, who is the same age, came from Barqa, a village on the Green Line, half in Israel and half in the occupied territory. Both still dreamt of returning home.

Now in their fifties, the two leading ideologues of holy war inspired a fresh generation to take on the powers that colonized the Muslim world and their local clients.

Al-Maqdisi's fatwas expanded Sayyid Qutb's application of *takfir*—excommunication for being an unbeliever—to Arab rulers, their advisors, and their armed forces, based on a Quranic verse from the Surat al-Qasas that states "and his ministers and soldiers." "Remove the tent-pegs and the tent will fall," he argued, reasoning that the Arab world was ruled by tyrannies, not tyrants. He grinned that he was the first to apply *takfir* to the Saudi ruling family.

Al-Maqdisi's many recruits include Abu Musab al-Zarqawi, a petty Palestinian criminal from Jordan's depressed urban sprawl of Zarqa whom he mentored in a Jordanian prison from 1995 to 1999. When they first met, al-Maqdisi recalls, Zarqawi's forearm was puckered with bruises from the drugs he injected. Al-Maqdisi rehabilitated him, inspiring him to launch al-Qaeda's branch in Iraq, the forerunner of the Islamic State.

Al-Maqdisi was not without some misgivings about the movement he spawned. Zarqawi had erred, he said, by extending the jihad to Shias, and he did not approve of attacks that inadvertently kill innocent Muslims. He showed me the fatwas and private letters he had sent Zarqawi urging him to stop suicide bombings on Shia marketplaces. His own lawyer is a New York Jew named Stanley Cohen.

Abu Qatada was less nuanced. In 1993, he had fled a death sentence in Jordan, and from the relative comfort of the leafy London suburb of Ealing, the armchair jihadi set about coining fresh rules of engagement. Branded al-Qaeda's man in Europe, he issued the fatwa that licensed the Armed Islamic Group, an Algerian jihadi organization, to kill the wives and children of Algerian soldiers and policemen in their mission to establish an Islamic state. Unlike the ideologues of the Muslim Brotherhood, who purport to heal Islam's differences with the West, Abu Qatada revels in the clash of civilizations. Preachers should not "pretend" Islam conforms to treaties of universal human rights—men were not born to be free but to be the slaves of God, he says. The philosophy did not hold him back

84   from using every available international human rights article to wage a ten-year-long battle against deportation from prison in Britain to Jordan. In 2013 he lost, and was sent back to Jordan to face charges of terrorism. He was acquitted in June 2014, the same month al-Maqdisi was released from his Jordanian cell after five years.

While many senior Muslim Brothers have doctorates, most jihadi leaders are self-taught. Al-Maqdisi and Abu Qatada never went to university. Their sermons are populist and idiosyncratic. Al-Maqdisi says he learned about political theory from the prison copy of Dan Brown's *The Da Vinci Code*. "It shows how religious states work," he says. Abu Qatada discovered America's underbelly in Jack London's *The Iron Heel*. Unlike the uptight Muslim Brothers, their humor is ribald and coarse. After years in prison, they are as obsessed with sex as boys from a boarding school. Theresa May, the British interior minister who deported Abu Qatada, is "from a whorehouse," says al-Maqdisi. Just out of prison, Abu Qatada complains he is too busy with his wife to find time to read. Jihadi fatwas discuss short-term marriages, "sharing women," and luring Muslim girls from the West for *jihad nikah*, or sexual jihad. As in the Prophet's time, soldiers of the jihad are far from home, and their libidos have to be satisfied. In a society struggling to balance the taboo on sex before marriage with the lack of means to afford a family home, the jihadis promise a release from frustration. Not only will they enjoy virgins in the hereafter, but the prospect of multiple unions in the here and now.

Al-Maqdisi and Abu Qatada's populist jihad prove well-placed to fill the vacuum left by the many failures of the civilian movements that initiated the Arab Spring. They mocked the Islamists who naively thought the ballot box an effective mechanism for taking power, not least Mohammed Badie, the Muslim Brotherhood's Supreme Guide, who called for restraint and non-violence after Abdel Fattah el-Sisi toppled the brotherhood's elected government, and was promptly sentenced to death. "Armed regimes do not so readily surrender power," says Abu Qatada. "Dialogue and compromise do not work. Look where it got him." From Oliver Cromwell's Commonwealth to the American Civil War, liberation movements only won through the barrel of the gun, he argued. "The Arab Spring has passed," he says. "The Arab world no longer believes in democracy. The Mujahideen Spring is coming—with blood." Today, a third of Iraq and Syria is in jihadi hands. Lebanon, Saudi Arabia, and Jordan, he predicts, would follow.

When they were in prison, al-Maqdisi and Abu Qatada had unreservedly denounced the Islamic State. Perhaps al-Maqdisi worried that as they aged, a younger, more radical generation was taking their place. The bulk of new jihadi recruits were joining IS's ranks, and from his sofa, al-Maqdisi found it hard to compete. But his animosity for IS's leader, Abu Bakr al-Baghdadi, was tempered by a personal connection. In Anbar and later in prison, al-Baghdadi had looked after al-Maqdisi's son, Omar. For a jihadi ideologue who had inspired many to go to their deaths, al-Maqdisi was openly grieving. Omar was killed in an ambush on his release from prison as he headed to Mosul to join his new wife, he told me. He kept showing me his photograph, as if struggling to comprehend the personal sacrifice his preaching had caused.

86   Thereafter al-Baghdadi and al-Maqdisi exchanged correspondence. "The Quran calls on Muslims to kill their enemies, not aid-workers," he had recently written. Al-Maqdisi should stop listening to lies from the Gulf's intelligence agencies, al-Baghdadi replied. The rebuff pained al-Maqdisi, and out of prison, he tweaked his messaging. Al-Baghdadi's forces might be wayward, but the coalition of Arab clients that America had assembled against them was worse.

    That al-Baghdadi could withstand the assault of a 60-nation alliance of apostates, crusaders, and Shias gave him a certain mystique.

The Islamic State

For almost a century Palestinians had been the handmaidens of global jihad. While other jihadi movements had fought local power struggles in Egypt, Syria, Algeria, and Libya, Palestinian mentors had laid the intellectual foundations. Palestinian commanders, like Zarqawi in Iraq and Abu Muhammad al-Julani, the leader of the al-Nusra Front in Syria, experimented with their theories.

But America's occupation of Iraq shifted jihad's center of gravity. No longer were Sunni militants struggling for peripheral places like Afghanistan or Somalia, but for Baghdad, the Arab world's heartland and former seat of the caliphate. Not only did America's rule resuscitate an age of direct colonialism, it also upended 1,400 years of Sunni domination of Shias in the Arab world. "Sunni Islam is under attack," protested a Jordanian juice-maker, typifying a popular

88   response to scenes of American tanks roling into Baghdad
"Ever since the second Gulf War, the West has been trying to
break Sunni power. We have to defend it."

Abu Bakr al-Baghdadi and the Caliphate

No sooner had Atatürk abolished the Ottoman caliphate in 1924
than Sunni revivalist movements began discussing its res-
urrection. At the World Islamic Congress in 1931, Haj Amin
al-Husseini, the grand mufti of Jerusalem, had tentatively nomi-
nated himself for caliph. Hassan al-Banna, the founder of the
Muslim Brotherhood, suggested selecting the candidate by con-
sensus. The pan-Islamic political organization Hizb ut-Tahrir
proposed launching the caliphate with a military coup. But thereafter the idea had lain dormant, too ambitious even for bin Laden.

Three weeks after his capture of Mosul, Iraq's second city,
a scholar of the Prophet's sayings took the step no other Arab
leader had dared for centuries and declared himself caliph. Abu
Bakr al-Baghdadi's realm encompassed the wellspring of the
world's civilization, the Euphrates and Tigris valleys, a territory
larger and richer than Jordan, with about eight million people
under his rule. But his aspirations were borderless. Denouncing
the sin of nationalism, he dropped the geographical references
in his group's name, and rebranded it simply the Islamic State.
By adopting the title of caliph, he had climbed above the status
of Kings Salman, Hamed, Abdullah, and Mohammed and
catapulted himself into the highest office in Islam.

Initially, some wondered whether he might serve as an
antidote to Zarqawi's vicious sectarianism and restore the

religious inclusivity the post had commanded in Ottoman times. Though his *nom de guerre*, Abu Bakr, had been the first Sunni caliph, he renamed himself Caliph Ibrahim, recalling Abraham, the father of all monotheistic faiths and also his original name, Ibrahim Awwad. His family, though Sunnis, came from Samarra, on the banks of the Tigris 60 miles north of Baghdad. For generations they had served as sweepers tending the forecourts of the city's great Shia shrines. Sunnis as well as Shias earned their keep from the pilgrimage, and inter-marriage was common. Moreover, the family's descent from the Prophet and their religious scholarship had won them the respect of Sunnis and Shias alike. One of Awwad's cousins, Abdelaziz al-Badri, founded the Iraqi branch of Hizb ut-Tahrir in the 1950s, which at the time attracted Shias as well as Sunnis with its call to sweep aside Arab nationalist regimes and replace them with a pan-Islamic caliphate. Some of this outlook might have rubbed off on al-Baghdadi. Unlike Zarqawi's rabid anti-Shiism, al-Baghdadi is said to have been sympathetic to Shia claims that Ali and his sons were robbed of the caliphate.

Such pluralism belonged to a past age. Long before America invaded, Saddam Hussein had fused nationalism and sect. During the Iran-Iraq War, Hussein had countered Ayatollah Khomeini's Shia revivalism by promoting his own credentials as a Sunni leader. To revive his flagging legitimacy after his rout in Kuwait, he launched a *hamla imaniya*, or faith campaign, banned the consumption (though not the non-Muslim sale) of alcohol in public spaces, closed nightclubs, turned the mosques into distribution centers for UN rations, and established a personal

90   militia, the Fedayeen Saddam, which patrolled the streets as a kind of religious police. Muslim women again donned the veil, resurrecting a separate dress code for non-Muslims, after decades in which differences blurred. He required Ba'ath Party members to pass a religious exam and stopped party meetings for prayers. With Saudi finance in 1988, he opened the Saddam University for Islamic Studies, a religious college with a large component of foreign students.

Ibrahim Awwad enrolled there to study the Quran in 1995 at a time when Saddam was recruiting Islamists in the struggle against America's coalition. He co-opted Sufi lodges and prevailed upon Salafis to open mosques across Iraq. With Hussein's blessing Arab jihadis fleeing America's bombardment of Afghanistan found refuge in Iraq's northern Kurdish mountains. As U.S. forces amassed in Kuwait in 2003, jihadis from across the region gravitated to Iraq's defense.

At first Awwad did not join them. But when American tanks parked at the intersection outside his mosque, something changed. He began preaching sermons at Abu Hanifa, Baghdad's most prestigious Sunni mosque, condemning not only the Americans but their Shia lackeys who had welcomed them. He blessed the mounting armed resistance, and on February 4, 2004, U.S. forces detained him and shipped him to Camp Bucca, a vast open-air prison with some 20,000 inmates on the edge of Basra, Iraq's southern port. The prison camp proved a particularly effective incubator for the Iraqi jihad. Ba'athists, Salafis, former army officers, and Sunni tribesmen spent the days debating, studying, and strategizing in identical yellow prison jumpsuits that emphasized their common predicament.

Though released after only six months for want of incriminating evidence, Awwad had remained in Camp Bucca for long enough to be noticed. Inmates remember him as a mild-mannered figure with a devoted following. Unlike most jihadi preachers, he had the authority of a classical education. From his study of narration in the Prophet's sayings, he acquired a knack for discerning tribal pedigrees and building alliances. On his release he returned to his doctorate at the renamed Iraqi University, assuming a mastery of religious sciences that other jihadis, including bin Laden and Zarqawi, never matched.

By night, Awwad became Abu Bakr al-Baghdadi, helping Zarqawi's group, al-Qaeda in Iraq, recruit and dispatch suicide bombers. The rapid turnover helped him advance up the hierarchy. American forces killed Zarqawi in 2006, and with other Sunni militant groups al-Baghdadi helped establish a new umbrella organization, the Islamic State in Iraq. Four years later, after further U.S. strikes on its leadership, al-Baghdadi was made the group's leader. Bolstered by some 350 jihadis after the jailbreak from Abu Ghraib prison in 2012, his fighters swept up the Euphrates River into Syria, filling the vacuum left by a Sunni revolt that had forced Bashar al-Assad's regime into retreat. With a third of Syria under his command by 2013, al-Baghdadi renamed his movement the Islamic State in Iraq and Syria and founded his capital in Raqqa, the summer seat of the most illustrious of the Abbasid caliphs, Haroun al-Rashid.

Had Iraq's prime minister, Nouri al-Maliki, not so cavalierly alienated Sunni public opinion, al-Baghdadi might never

92   have repeated his success in Iraq. In 2008, America's generals persuaded Iraq's Sunni tribes to switch sides and chase out al-Qaeda with the offer of arms, training, and finance. Known as the Sahwa (awakening), the program at its peak counted 90,000 tribesmen. But where the Americans had embraced Sunni tribes, al-Maliki considered their sheer size a threat. He stripped the tribes of their stipends, and appointed his loyalists in their stead.

Sunni Arabs erupted in protests that were remarkable for their absence of violence. They owed much to similar scenes shaking Tunis and Cairo, and continued despite crackdowns and show trials for corruption that al-Maliki ordered. Only after a year of demonstrations did Sunni activists despair of civil resistance and looked elsewhere. When IS drove into Mosul on June 9, 2014, a resident recalls people welcoming them with flowers, as if Saddam Hussein had returned.

In both Raqqa and Mosul, al-Baghdadi gained control by negotiating alliances and employing shock tactics, rather than engage in actual fighting. Unlike Hamas and al-Qaeda, which used suicide bombing against civilian targets, the next generation of jihadis turned suicide bombing into an offensive weapon and launched convoys of armored vehicles laden with explosives at enemy lines. Their supply of would-be suicide bombers seemed limitless. Brides were known to write a commitment to martyrdom into their marriage contracts. Hamas had spent months preparing recruits; jihadi groups in Iraq and Syria boasted a turnaround time of two weeks. The chosen candidates were always the newest recruits. Veterans would hug and congratulate the designated martyr and hail him as a hero. The peer pressure was hard to resist, and war pensions offered a further incentive. With few job prospects, young men were worth more to their families dead than alive.

Such was the fear IS aroused that by the time its fighters had driven the 100 kilometers from the Syrian border to Mosul, the Iraqi army commanders in Ghuzlani, the country's largest training camp in the north, had fled in helicopters. Leaderless soldiers threw away their uniforms and left for Kurdistan without firing a shot. Some local Sunnis simply switched sides, taking their weapons with them. The few that held out were too disorientated by truck bombs to coordinate their defense. With a few dozen pickup trucks, IS captured 2,300 armored cars and hundreds of millions of dollars of munitions.

As panic spread, Kurdish *peshmergas* retreated from the Nineveh plains without notice, abandoning Yazidis and Christians to their fate. A contingent of a few dozen militants in seven vehicles seized Tikrit in an afternoon. Cowed and perhaps wowed by IS's success, other cities down the Tigris and Euphrates pledged their allegiance. Iraq's security forces, on which over $100 billion had been lavished between 2006 and 2014, simply melted away. Within a week the Sunni Arab advance had reached the outskirts of Baghdad.

Mosul was al-Baghdadi's greatest prize. The money from its bank vaults and its oil fields turned IS into the world's wealthiest terrorist organization. Salary payments to its fighters exceeded those of soldiers in many regional armies, attracting jihadis from Tangier to Tashkent. But IS also won local support. Known as the city of officers, Mosul's martial tradition dated back to the Assyrians. Its officer class had formed the backbone of Saddam Hussein's army. And many rallied to al-Baghdadi, hoping he would revive the city's lost glory, dating back to 1920 when its elders tried to keep their status as a satrap inside Turkey rather than surrender their autonomy to Baghdad. With Baghdad under shared American and Shia control after 2003 the resentment had only increased. Few Maslawis had shown much interest in al-Qaeda when it made its first bid for control of the city in 2006; far more rallied to IS's cause in 2014.

Brimming with confidence, IS claimed to banish corruption, opened Mosul's prisons, removed the web of grindingly slow checkpoints that had turned a ten-minute trip to the town center into a two-hour jam, and initially facilitated unfettered travel to neighboring Turkey. "We're free," celebrated a retired engineer. The dress code initially seemed disarmingly relaxed. Men could go out in public clean-shaven, and women with no more than a simple headscarf. IS forces, which included a significant contingent of foreigners, kept their distance and left locals, particularly tribesmen from surrounding villages, to police the city.

The various Sunni groups America's invasion had disenfranchised—tribal leaders, Salafis, Sufis, Ba'athists, former army officers—prepared for another marriage of convenience. Al-Baghdadi's second in command was a member of Saddam Hussein's military intelligence unit. A second deputy was a major general in the Iraqi army. IS assimilated much of Ba'athism's state ideology as well as its manpower. In place of the Ba'ath party's idealized unified Arab state, it constructed an idealized unified Islamic one, destined to usher in a renaissance, and transform the Sunni sect into the nation-state of

Islam. With echoes of the right of return Israel extended to Jews, it promoted the ingathering of Sunnis worldwide into the caliphate. Its methods seemed similarly lifted from Ba'ath manuals. IS used fear as a tool of control in a one-party, totalitarian state. Saddam's cohorts graduated by killing a dog with their hands; IS cadres had to kill a prisoner. They filmed their victims digging their own graves, as the Nazis did. Both called their youth movements *al-ashbal*, or lion cubs.

If bin Laden was Islam's answer to Trotsky, an elitist who dissipated al-Qaeda's energies fighting enemies across the globe, al-Baghdadi was Islam's Stalin, a populist focused on establishing a territorial base in the heartlands. As the Kurds had their regional government in Erbil, and the Shia their grand ayatollahs in Najaf, so the caliphate furnished Iraq's Sunnis with a long-awaited center of gravity.

On the third Friday prayers after IS's Mosul takeover, the naïvete of the optimists who had foreseen a new era of inclusiveness became apparent. Preachers declared Christians should leave, pay a monthly *jizya* of $300, or face death. Like Jews in the 1950s, those who opted to leave were fleeced on departure. IS fighters took over abandoned churches, cleansed them of crucifixes and icons whose half-naked figurines offended IS's sensibilities, and left their furniture on the roadsides for Sunnis to claim as booty. They pinned black standards to the church steeples and used them as shelters, correctly assuming America's coalition would spare them bombardment. A community as old as the Bible, 175,000 strong, shriveled to virtually none. "We've reached the end of Christianity in Iraq," says Ghazi

96   al-Rahu, who took refuge in Jordan, where King Abdullah agreed
to admit a few thousand Iraqi Christians.

Worse was in store. Shias, who made up 10 percent of
Mosul's population, joined the exodus. And in August, IS
forces advanced on the Yazidis' holy mountain of Sinjar. Some
750,000 Yazidis took flight, but not before thousands of Yazidi
women had been abducted and their husbands and fathers
killed. "Spoils of war," IS's English-language magazine, *Dabiq*,
called them. Islam permitted sex with non-Muslim "slaves,"
including pre-pubescent girls, enjoined a fatwa. *Dabiq* quoted a
companion of the Prophet as saying that "approaching any married woman is fornication, except for a woman who has been
enslaved." Two of the Prophet's wives, it noted, were Jewish
spoils of war, and Imam Ali had 19 slave girls. "I and those with
me at home prostrated to Allah in gratitude on the day the first
slave-girl entered our home," added *Dabiq*'s supposed female
author, Umm Sumayyah. Others cited the Quranic chapter called "The Women," in which the Quran sanctioned the
marriage of up to four wives, or "those that your right hand pos-
sesses." Slave markets reopened after a century-long lapse.

The mass rape that ensued was not just barbarous lust,
but a systematic weapon of war and part of IS's program of
cultural erasure. "The aim is. . . humiliation of whoever desires
a religion other than Islam!" explained *Dabiq*. Destroy family
units, shroud communities in shame, and capture, control, and
convert their means of reproduction, and Yazidism would be
erased forever and a new world of homogeneity rise in its place.

For all the hype surrounding minorities the prime target of
IS was its Sunni population. It sought to purify them of cultural

impurities and hone them into holy warriors equipped for regaining lost Sunni lands. A month into their rule, IS forces destroyed Mosul University's chemistry labs and closed the departments of antiquities, arts, law, political science, and philosophy. Their bureaucrats introduced the curriculum used in Saudi secondary schools almost in its entirety. *Torshe*, pickled vegetables, were banned since the vinegar used might have come from wine. To encourage men to grow their beards IS banned barbers not just from shaving beards but trimming them too. It first required women to cover the upper body with a low-hanging *himar*, or veil, and then to don face-coverings and gloves too. Prepubescent girls, between ages six and nine, wore white veils, and could show their faces. Any girl older was required to wear black. The streets became as uniform as the faith, "full of moving black tents," complained a lecturer at Mosul University, whose male students one day began wearing Afghan dress. Women could drive, an improvement on Saudi Arabia, but only—somewhat dangerously—with their faces covered. Offenders were pulled aside at checkpoints and stripped of their ID cards, which they could only recover on payment of a fine at the new sharia courts. Taxi drivers caught driving women without a male *mahram*, or guardian, incurred a fine of $42. Women were banned from leaving their homes during Ramadan.

Suspected homosexuals were pushed from the rooftops of high-rises. Stories circulated of a child whose fingers were severed for smoking and of a doctor decapitated for failing to resuscitate an injured fighter.

To fashion their brave new world, IS purged not only Mosul's pluralist present but its past. The Naqshabandi Sufi order had initially backed al-Baghdadi's takeover, but acolytes were subjected to reeducation. Their lodges were demolished. Other shrines and mosques built in graveyards were deemed to compromise the absolute worship of one God and accordingly "removed" and "torched." Over a dozen medieval mosques in Mosul were leveled. The Nithamiya, the city's twelfth-century Seljuk madrassa, was toppled on the erroneous grounds that it contained a shrine to Ali al-Asghar, the youngest child of the third Shia imam Husayn ibn Ali. Mosul's public library and theater were set alight.

"We're spreading monotheism across the planet," celebrated one of IS's henchmen as he took a drill to a *lamassu*, one of the colossal statues of human-headed winged bulls that guarded Assyrian temples. Behind him, the faithful invoked Abraham's name and sledgehammered, bulldozed, and detonated the eighth-century BCE citadel of Sargon II. Amir al-Jumaili, an antiquities professor at Mosul University, recorded the destruction of some 160 ancient sites before fleeing the city, and showed me his diary entries:

5 March 2015—Nimrud attacked

6 March 2015—Hatra attacked

9 March 2015—Khorsabad attacked

The scale was unprecedented. Four of Syria's six world heritage sites had been damaged when IS seized a fifth, Palmyra, an ancient city renowned in classical times for its pluralism. When its retired 83-year-old chief of antiquities refused to divulge where the site's treasures were stashed, IS had him publicly beheaded and his body hung from a traffic light. Appeals for international intervention were met with hand-wringing. In

March 2015, Iraq's distraught archaeologists and antiquities experts gathered for a closed government-sponsored conference in Baghdad. Iraq had 12,000 archaeological sites—too many to protect, said Ahmed Kamel, the balding, bespectacled director of the National Museum of Iraq, which houses the country's greatest collection of antiquities. (It was looted under America's watch 12 years earlier.) His sole source of comfort was that 90 percent of Mosul province's 1,763 sites had yet to be properly excavated. Some of the experts proposed promoting a resolution at the UN Security Council calling for the U.S.-led coalition to protect heritage sites. Others advocated the creation of a national antiquities guard. Iraq's national security advisor, Faleh Fayadh, promised to consider this, and then nodded off during a presentation about the temple to the sun god at Hatra, which IS had also attacked.

In the conference hall, some of the delegates were crying. *"La howla wal la quwa,"* they mumbled (there's no power [but God's]), as a projector relayed scenes of medieval minarets tumbling, and Mosul's landmark, the dome of Nabi Yunus, collapsing in ruins. IS fighters erased Nimrud, the ancient Assyrian capital, with a chain of explosives, and fired machine guns at the Gorgon heads that graced the palaces. Tears made tracks in the presenter's makeup. "They are trying to destroy a people's identity," said Fayadh, briefly roused from his slumber.

Archaeologists offered an explanation for IS's rampage. Since the nineteenth century they had sought the rulers' permission to dig beneath Nabi Yunus in the hope of uncovering the mythical throne room of the Assyrian rulers. Perhaps, they speculated, it might house the loot Sargon II captured when he

100   destroyed the Kingdom of Israel in the eighth century BCE and carted its ten tribes into captivity. The Ottoman governor had refused to let Sir Austen Henry Layard, an archaeologist from the British Museum, excavate in the 1860s, lest he violate the site's Islamic sanctity. IS's new caliph had no such qualms. Two days after destroying Nabi Yunus, IS summoned al-Jumaili, the antiquities professor, and his colleagues to survey the rubble. "They are digging, not just destroying," he said. Behind their lofty pretensions to defend monotheism lurked bounty hunters and tomb raiders.

By the same token, al-Jumaili reasoned that the video IS produced of the destruction of Mosul's antiquities museum in February 2015 was designed to trigger international outrage, inflate demand, and jack up prices of those artifacts that survived. Many of the exhibits in the Hatra Hall were reproductions, but of its 30 original pieces, he said that the jihadis had hacked at ten. Footage from the priceless exhibits in the prehistoric, Islamic, and Assyrian halls was absent. Whole warehouses, he had heard from Turkish sources, were full of their loot. Using satellite imagery, the Washington-based AAAS Geospatial Technologies Project traced a five-fold increase in digs along the Euphrates Valley after IS took control. It counted 3,750 looting pits outside the walls of Dura-Europos alone, a third-century BCE Syrian trading hub. In the 50-hectare area within the walls, there were too many to count. An Iraqi government advisor estimated that mining heritage sites in Iraq and Syria had become the caliphate's most lucrative source of finance after oil. Its cadresused earth-diggers to uncover the prime sites, while assigning lesser sites to individuals who paid a 20 percent cut of their earnings, sanctimoniously dubbed a khoms, or Islamic tithe. "The buying and selling of artifacts is what finances the beheadings," says an American official. Half-jokingly, Arab intellectuals appealed to Western museums to resume their colonial-age plunder, if only to ensure the safekeeping of antiquities. Let them steal our artifacts," bemoaned Abdel Rahman al-Rashed, one of the Arab world's most prominent journalists. "We do not deserve them."

IS found fresh ways to raise funds locally, too, establishing a rudimentary tax base, and introduced a lucrative system of fines. It established its own currency, issued certificates for import duties (which for a time Jordan treated as tax-deductible), and charged exit taxes, ending the free passage to Turkey and profiting from the flight of an estimated half-million of Mosul's two million people. Graffiti daubed on empty properties warned residents who abandoned their homes that they would be deemed *murtad,* or apostates, if they failed to return within an allotted timeframe and would forfeit their property. A policeman who fled his hometown of Hit in Anbar province after its capture by IS received a photo on his mobile phone of his house. The word *waqf,* or Islamic endowment, had been scrawled on its walls. "Saudis, Tunisians have taken it over," he told me. Its contents had been impounded or sold.

Curiously, foreign Islamists were spared much of the hardship. They received perks for relocating. In its 2015 manual for women, IS contrasts its favorable treatment of foreigners with those of the "hypocritical states" of the Gulf, where foreigners are obligated to pay a residency tax (*iqamah*) as if they were People of the Book, as if they are not equal to the people of the country in work, in healthcare, in social life and everything else. To hell with these laws, to hell with nationalism! Instead of this, in my state here, the Chechen is a friend of a Syrian, the Hijazi a neighbor of a Kazakh. Lineages are mixed, tribes merged and races joined under the banner of monotheism, resulting in a new generation integrating the cultures of many different peoples into a beautiful and harmonious alliance.

Foreign fighting elites were nothing new to Iraq. The Ottomans relied on Janissaries, emancipated Balkan slaves. The Abbasids had brought the Turks. But IS's determination to construct a new community based on sect was remarkable nonetheless. According to Iraqi prime minister Haider al-Abadi, by 2015 foreigners made up 60 percent of IS's fighting force. The largest component stemmed from North Africa and Saudi Arabia, but Europeans and Central Asians came in their thousands, too. The head of Tajikistan's counter-terrorism police unit declared his allegiance to the caliphate. In Mosul's upmarket district, Josak, locals complain that English and French are more widely spoken than Arabic.

Sameh Dhu al-Kurnain, a dual German and Egyptian national who heads Mosul's education department for the IS, perplexingly kept the English department open but closed the French department, which the great orientalist Louis Massignon helped establish in the early 1950s. Despite his own foreign education, he banned Iraqis from studying abroad. "In the land

of the caliphate we need *mujahideen*, not doctorates from the
land of the *kuffar*,"—that is, jihadis and not unbelievers—he
explained when a medic sought an exit permit.

"So how come you have a German doctorate?" the medic
bravely rejoined.

"I left my wife, I left Germany, and married jihad," al-
Kurnain said, suggesting the medic do the same.

Counter-strike

With scant means to unseat IS themselves, some Sunni tribal
elders responded to al-Abadi's efforts to revive the Sahwa force
of Sunni tribesmen his predecessor dissolved. Concerned for
the fate of their tribal lands in the event of a government victory, tribal elders sent their representatives to Baghdad's once
luxury Al Mansour Hotel in the spring of 2015 to declare their
allegiance to the Baghdad government, provided that any territory it recovered from IS reverted to their control.

But government officials had an unnerving way of talk-
ing about the liberation of Mosul, as if the battle was already
won. Dates for a promised counter-attack came and went. The
new Sahwa's numbers didn't quite stack up. In Tikrit, Saddam
Hussein's hometown, 110 miles from Baghdad, 400 IS fighters
held out against a 24,000-strong force for two months. Only
after Americans began aerial bombardments did IS finally stage
a retreat.

For all the official bravado, a victory parade in Mosul
seemed a less-than-immediate prospect. IS forces in Mosul are
some 25 times more than those in Tikrit, and are readily

104   reinforced from Syria. As if doubting the likelihood of an early conquest, even the Americans focused their bombings on IS's edges, stemming their further advance rather than threatening their nerve centers.

Nor, for all their trepidation of IS, is it clear that most Sunnis favor such an assault. Many have learned to mistrust promises of liberation since the Americans first marched into Iraq, fearing it might just herald a fresh bout of sectarian cleansing. When propounding his plans for retaking Mosul, Iraq's prime minister insists he has the backing of Baghdad's Abu Hanifa Mosque, the base of the capital's Sunni clerical establishment. But when I went to see them, its clerics sounded unconvinced. "Why should militiamen from Basra in the south invade a city in the north?" asks the mosque's spokesman Taha Hamid al-Zaydi, who once studied with al-Baghdadi. "It will simply make matters worse." His rhetorical questions suggest a latent sympathy with Mosul's new order. "What is more important, killing a human or the toppling of stones?" he asks when I protest IS's destruction of some of the world's oldest antiquities. "Only mosques built over graves have been destroyed."

Each time I try to talk to him about IS, he lists the crimes the Shia-dominated government in Baghdad continues to commit against Sunnis. In their conquest of Tikrit, Shia forces separated men and women, raping the latter and killing the former. "Life is normal in Mosul," al-Zaydi says. "People of Mosul are more afraid of the future than of the present. We fear huge massacres to come." As we leave, my driver tells me that al-Zaydi's underlings in the corridor had joked about how much ransom I might fetch.

Although Shia militias pushed IS out of three central provinces—Diyala, Saladin, and by December 2015, most of Al Anbar—its forces quickly regrouped. Like a game of whack-a-mole, IS's position astride the Syrian-Iraqi border helps it vanish from one town only to surface in another. No sooner had it retreated from Tikrit than it entered the southern suburbs of Damascus. Despite 11,000 coalition bombing raids, some with B-52s, IS proved not just its staying power, but its capacity to expand. In May 2015, it took Ramadi, the provincial capital of Anbar, and the Syrian city of Palmyra, replete with two gas fields, the country's largest phosphate mine, and one of the world's richest sites for antiquities smuggling. With its $1 billion of revenues, it withstood the impact of America's $580 billion military budget and brought the 60-nation coalition to what Martin Dempsey, then chairman of the Joint Chiefs of Staff, called a "tactical stalemate." "We're just tinkering at the edges," complained an American diplomat of the 12 air raids the coalition launched every night.

Many IS subjects who had known no rule but tyranny were resigned to swapping one dictatorship for another. And once they had paid their hefty fees, IS rule had some advantages. It offered more internal security and absence of corruption than many other parts of devastated Syria. There were no rival militias all levying separate fees. Economists at a Beirut conference in mid-2015 voted IS-held territory Syria's best performing. Due to fear and a functioning court system, crime was exceptionally rare. Indeed, so miserable were conditions for Iraq's internally displaced that some 200,000 Iraqis returned to IS-controlled territory.

106   For all the vitriol its followers spouted against Shias, the IS's medium-term goal seemed to be consolidation of its grip on Sunni communities, not the conquest of Shia ones. Possibly on account of his family background, al-Baghdadi made no mention of Shias in his sermon assuming the caliphate. He issued passes for Shia truck drivers to transport his oil. In Syria, he cut deals with the Assad regime, though he deemed the Alawite creed of its leader a form of unbelief punishable by death. He devoted more effort to fighting rival Sunni movements than Shia ones. Mecca, with all its material, political, and religious riches, was more of a target. IS propagandists highlight the differences between the Islamic State and the "Hypocritical State" of the Al Sauds, who had ridden the coattails of ibn Abd al-Wahhab's forces to win a kingdom but had now prostituted their realm to the West. In April 2015, fighters in Anbar made their first cross-border raid into Saudi Arabia, and a month later began a campaign of destabilization with the bombing of Shia mosques in the kingdom. Its soft power was even more striking than its 70,000-stong force. In an online poll conducted in July 2014, 92 percent of Saudi citizens agreed that IS "conforms to the values of Islam." Further afield, it proved adept at establishing a foothold in ungoverned spaces like Derna and Sirte in Libya, Sinai in Egypt, the so-called Khorasan Province on the Afghan-Pakistani border, the North Caucasus, and Yemen. That's not to mention pledges of allegiance from Jund al-Khilafah in Algeria, Boko Haram in Nigeria, and Abu Sayyaf in the Philippines.

Perceived betrayals by Sunni monarchs and presidents have compounded hitherto scattered Sunni grievances and consolidated them into an increasingly solid vexatious rump.

For all its horror, the explosive ascendancy of what began as a branch of al-Qaeda in Iraq has inspired many Sunnis, especially those who saw their sect becoming more and more marginalized. Regardless of whether IS's forces themselves can be overcome, left unaddressed, Sunni grievances will likely find expression again, perhaps in a yet more terrible guise.

The Creation of Shiastan

Part Four

Hashad

The grand ayatollah's little lecture hall in Najaf is as shabby and dilapidated as it was in the days of Saddam Hussein. Material upgrades, the peeling paint seems to suggest, might compromise the spirituality of the *hawza*, the center of Shia learning in the southern Iraqi city. Crosslegged on a threadbare carpet, 100 turbaned men hang on the words of the squat figure crouched slightly above them in a makeshift wooden armchair several sizes too big for him. A camera recording his lecture on the Islamic laws of bartering is Grand Ayatollah Sayyid al-Hakim's only compromise with modernity.

While the scholars are disciplined with monastic conditions, the *hoi polloi* are dazzled with the opulence of the Imam Ali Mosque. In his office above the commotion, the shrine's treasurer, Zuhair Sharba, maps the progress on a $600 million expansion, set to swell the shrine's capacity fivefold. Appropriately enough, since pilgrimage is the city's prime income generator, he is also chair of Najaf's chamber of commerce. He banks the tithes that the world's 200 million Shias raise worldwide for the city's ayatollahs, and much of the income that 30 flights of pilgrims a day generate. A dozen cranes rotate above the holy site, industrial spiders weaving a web of luxury hotels, fountained courtyards, a towering media city, and accommodation for a student intake that has quadrupled since Saddam's downfall. The city is the most flourishing and peaceful in Iraq.

Puncturing this splendid isolation, a new funeral cortege arrives at the shrine's thresholds every few minutes and unloads a fresh cadaver. Each makeshift coffin is wrapped in the costume of a military funeral—Iraqi flags made in China stuck on with sticky tape. Relatives snuffle; fellow fighters stare blankly ahead, awaiting their turn. In much the same way as Iran's former Supreme Leader, Ayatollah Ruhollah Khomeini, blocked Saddam Hussein's eight-year invasion with human waves, so Najaf's ayatollahs unleashed droves of Shia poor to stem IS's sweep south. "We know we're going to die," an armchair apologist with a UNESCO seat in religious studies at the local university told me. "We go to the front as if on a pilgrimage." The editor of a local periodical, *al-Asala*, is more circumspect: "The clerics don't send their sons to the front," he scowls. "They send the poor."

For over a decade, Ali Sistani, the foremost of Najaf's four grand ayatollahs, struck a pacifist's pose. When Sunni suicide bombers targeted Shia rites, he refused to call Shias to arms. When others demanded revenge, he called for elections. When militants blew the dome off Samarra's al-Askari Shrine, he warned against descending into civil war. Critics said that he was unable to shrug off the mindset of centuries of submission to Sunni powers, well-honed under Saddam Hussein, when deference was the best defense mechanism. He called it righteous restraint.

Abu Bakr al-Baghdadi, IS's caliph, succeeded where other Sunni emirs had failed in rousing him into battle. Ten days after al-Baghdadi's capture of Mosul, with IS closing on Baghdad and openly threatening to storm Najaf, Sistani issued a call for "citizens to defend the country, its people, the honor of its citizens, and its sacred places." Delighted militiamen hailed it a fatwa for jihad. In their panic, cloistered clerics morphed into militant mullahs. A Shia preacher from Qatar, Nazar al-Qatari, wearing military fatigues, called on worshippers to fight "the slayers of Imams Hasan and Hussein"—an oblique reference to Sunnis—and enlist in the *hashad shaabi,* or popular mobilization. As I walked out of the shrine with a businessman, his five-year-old son pulled on his father's arm and asked daddy to buy him a pistol.

In their antechambers, the clerics gave vent to a long pent-up sectarianism. "IS is nothing new," an advisor to Sistani told me. "Sunnis might sometimes have worn a suit and tie, but they have been killing Shias from the beginning." Rather than find explanations for IS's rise in the exclusive policies Iraq's Shia leaders had pursued, they traced the violence to something brutal and innate in Sunni Islam. Shia television preachers lambasted Sunnis for the three usurpers, or *nawasib,* who "raped the *wilaya,*" or reign, the Prophet had bequeathed to his son-in-law, Ali. The third caliph, Omar ibn al-Khattab, regarded by Sunnis as a pinnacle of virtue, was the most treacherous of all, a thug who broke open the Prophet's front door, smashing the ribs of Fatima (the Prophet's daughter and wife of Imam Ali), who had been standing behind it, causing the abortion of her child Abdel Mohsin.

Omar's followers had maintained the tradition. Saladin, the Sunni hero who vanquished the Crusaders in the twelfth century, was no less a butcher of Shias than IS. He had overthrown the Shia caliphate of the Fatimids, conquered their capital, Cairo, and converted the world's first university, al-Zahra, named after the Prophet's daughter, into a bastion of Sunni orthodoxy renamed in its masculine form as al-Azhar. "He left Cairo's backstreets knee-deep in Shia blood," a cleric told me, as if recounting a recent news bulletin. "He burned libraries and universities and destroyed two million books. He turned Islam into a religion of killing." His name should not be Saladin, literally the reformer of religion, scoffed a colleague, but Kharab al-Din, the destroyer of religion.

By transitioning from passivity to activism or from submission to power, Arab Shiism was undergoing a form of Sunnization. Under Ottoman rule, Shias had been denied their own millet and subjugated under Sunnis. But as they consolidated their hold over central and southern Iraq, they assumed the same prerogatives Sunnis had enjoyed for centuries. For the first time since the overthrow of the Fatimids and Buyids a millennia earlier, mainstream Shiism ruled a state in the Arab world. With their newfound hubris, many struck incalcitrant positions. There was no room for negotiating with terrorists, one of Sistani's advisors told me, insisting with almost Israeli logic that "we don't have a Sunni partner." Ezzedin al-Hakim, the grand ayatollah's son, would lecture me for hours on the necessity for inter-religious dialogue, but rule out the prospects for an inter-denominational one. When he spoke of the battle against IS, he thought less of rescuing Sunni countrymen from IS's totalitarian rule than of the climactic turning point of an epic 1,400-year-old schism.

The Shias' assumption of power challenged not only the sectarian order but the divine order as well. For the previous four centuries the trajectories of Persian and Arab Shias had been at loggerheads. While Shiism was the state faith of Iran's shahs, it was considered a near heresy in Sunni-ruled Iraq. Living under Sunni rule in Najaf, Shia clerics fashioned theories that defensively deemed all rule after the twelfth imam abandoned the world as illegitimate, while their Persian counterparts increasingly posited the assumption of power for themselves. One scholar even referred to Iran's rulers as deputies of the ayatollahs. At the turn of the nineteenth century, the Shia jurist Mulla Ahmad Naraqi coined the first tractates discussing *wilayat al-faqih*, or theocratic rule of the jurist. Ayatollah Khomeini put theory into practice 160 years later with his Islamic revolution in Iran. Now that Iraqi Shias, too, were ruling themselves for the first time in a millennia, Najaf's traditional theories propounded by Sistani looked increasingly anachronistic.

Sistani's sway over Iraq's 40 separate Shia militias had long been tenuous. Many took their arms and funding from Iran, and openly declared their allegiance to their paymaster, Khomeini's successor, Supreme Leader Ali Khamenei. For form's sake, they still paid Sistani and his Najaf clerics lip service, but argued with a degree of religious gymnastics that while they followed his spiritual pronouncements, they heeded political statements from Tehran. Some disdained Sistani's traditionalism, cherry-picking more modern fatwas. While Sistani railed against satellite television on account of the surfeit of sexual imagery, one militia commander preferred the opinion of Ayatollah Mohammad Hussein Fadlallah, Lebanon's leading cleric who died in 2010 and deemed pornography acceptable for men who otherwise struggled to satisfy their wives. Others protested the backing Sistani appeared to give the American assault on Najaf in 2004 to oust the followers of a junior cleric, Muqtada al-Sadr, who had taken up arms against both the occupation and its clerical apologists.

But after a decade of tension, Sistani's fatwa narrowed the gap with his detractors. Shia militia commanders who had hitherto denounced Sistani's vacillation celebrated his de facto legalization of the militias' advance, proclaimed themselves his loyal subjects, and relished a new crop of recruits and government finance—worth $2.3 billion, said Iraq's prime minister. Not even Khomeini had dared to declare such an open-ended jihad, waxed Abu Jaafar al-Darraji, a senior commander running recruitment for the Badr Organization, the largest and most openly pro-Iranian of the militias. He pointed at the portraits he had pinned of Sistani throughout his vast indoor training center overlaid with stencils of guns. For the first time since the ninth century, when the twelfth Shia imam went into hiding, he celebrated, the Shia world's luminaries had authorized a jihad not just for self-defense, but expansion.

It was false praise. Sistani was credited with much that he never said. Though dubbed the fatwa of jihad, his ruling had not mentioned the word. And it stipulated that any *hashad*, or mobilization, be "sufficient," that is, limited in place and time, not open-ended. Moreover, al-Darraji had no intention of taking his orders from Sistani. From his office sofa, he pointed at a portrait Iran's Supreme Leader, Ayatollah Ali Khamenei, gruffly perched over his desk. "He's our *wali amr al-muslimeen*, the legal ruler in all the Muslim lands," hc said. The walls of the indoor training camp at the back of his office were lined with vast images of Khamenei and Sistani, side by side as if complementing each other. Asked if he was betraying his country, al-Darraji insisted that sectarian ties took precedence. There are, he explained, "no borders between Muslims, or between Arabs and Persians, except in faith." More powerful, disciplined, and effective than the national army, he insisted, the *hashad* would survive its battle with IS and form Iraq's counterpart to Iran's Basij, the paramilitary youth group Ayatollah Ruhollah Khomeini had founded in 1979 to defend Iran's revolution and uphold its religious mores. "The current government doesn't represent Islam," al-Darraji insisted. It should accept the Supreme Leader's leadership.

The threats were only part bombast. The deputy chief of Iraq's *hashad* was an Iranian-Iraqi dual national called Abu Mahdi al-Mohandis who reported directly to Iran's Revolutionary Guard. For decades he had worked as an Iranian agent targeting America's interests in the Gulf. He was blacklisted on Washington's terror list for masterminding the bombing of the American and French embassies in Kuwait in 1983. And when U.S. forces in Iraq tried to capture him in 2007,

116   he had fled to Iran. To ward off the threat to Baghdad from the
Sunni north, his forces had overrun the capital from the Shia
south. He shared Baghdad's government enclave, the Green
Zone, with the American embassy.

Conscious, perhaps, of the genie he had unleashed, Sistani
made an attempt to curb increasingly public excesses. A video
apparently showing hospital orderlies watching while Shia
militiamen beat a Sunni man to death in a hospital in the
Baghdad suburb of Kadhimiya went viral. Reports of looting
were rife, and news broadcasts relayed Shia beheadings of
captured IS fighters. Sistani dispatched middle-ranking clerics
to monitor the front lines and teach the hawza's rules of war.
"Do not pray in the house of a stranger if you can pray in the
street, " said one bound for Tikrit. "But if there's a threat of
snipers then you can enter. If food is on the table and it's going
to decay, you can eat it, as long as you pay for what you eat."
But discipline proved harder to maintain on the battlefield than
in Najaf's mannered cloisters. "I saw them looting armchairs in
Saladin province," complained a cleric after a trip to the front. "I
made them put them back, but who knows what happened once
my back was turned."

Though the Badr Organization's commanders might
not have been listening, Sistani earned unexpected support
from his erstwhile foe Muqtada al-Sadr. Over the course of a
decade his messianic militia, the Mahdi's Army, had mellowed,
resurfacing as Saraya al-Salam, or peacekeepers. They committed
to protect Sunnis and Shias from each other, and banned their
cadres from sporting bushy beards and wearing military fatigues
when off-duty. "The positives of the *hashad* have become

negatives," Sayid Ibrahim, a Baghdadbased leader of the Sadrist
Movement, told me. He criticized the *hashad* for not submitting
to the command of the defense ministry and lambasted its habit
of burning houses, stealing cars, and indulging in random killing.
Having defended Iraq against America's occupation, some
Sadrists wondered whether the time might come when they
would have to do the same against Iran's.

But reestablishing Shia factional support for a national
army required overcoming generations of mistrust. In its
80-year history, the country had only one Shia chief of staff,
Abdul-Wahid Shannan ar-Ribat. And even after 2003, the
defense ministry had remained a nominally Sunni fief. A new
force Shia-led from the outset seemed more reliable. Either
way, able to outgun and outman the formal army and with
far higher morale, the *hashad*'s 40 militias, almost all of Shia
extraction, had no intention of ceding control to a weaker
force. Able to field 23,000 men on the front lines and almost
100,000 more in reserves, they asserted their presence both
on and behind the front lines. While some led the assault on
IS, others consolidated their hold on the territories they retook
from IS, and operated as a home guard in the main government-
held cities enforcing strict social codes. Despite an official
ban on paramilitary operations away from the front, reservists
moved onto the streets as auxiliaries to the local police. Vans
without side windows and license plates waited in side streets,
apparently to take suspects away. Sunnis were a particular
target.

In the towns ringing Baghdad, the *hashad* engaged in fresh
bouts of sectarian cleansing, turning much of the capital's

118   environs into Sunni-free zones. The perpetrators called them settlers, put there by Saddam Hussein to dilute and control Shia populations, though many had roots dating back centuries. They posed a security threat, insisted a militia commander who rejected in writing Prime Minister al-Abadi's order that Sunnis be allowed to return. Had they not provided the pool of suicide bombers and fired the mortars that preyed upon pilgrims? he asked. If the Shia holy shrines were to be spared repeated attack, Sunnis residing near pilgrimage routes from Baghdad and Iran should be removed.

"What can the prime minister do?" asked Sunni tribal leader and politician Mudher al-Janabi. "He's not in charge." Inside his fortified villa in Baghdad, he nervously eyed the bank of monitors on his desk relaying footage from the security cameras installed on the high walls surrounding his house. He had promised his tribe to lead them home to Jurf al-Sakhar, a village just south of Baghdad, but despaired of ever doing so. The irrigation system piping water from the Euphrates to his villagers' farmland had been broken and no one had bothered to fix it. Baghdad's breadbasket had turned into caked scrub. Three thousand Sunni homes in Jurf al-Sakhar had been destroyed, a parliamentary committee had reported, and a further 2,000 rendered uninhabitable. Thirteen Sunni villages around Sherwan, near the Iranian border, had been leveled entirely and turned into military zones to provide unfettered access from Iran. Even if the army had wanted to protect Sunni residents, militiamen barred their path.

To prevent the flight of displaced Sunnis further south, Shia provincial governors imposed entry restrictions, barring entry to those without local sponsors. Henchmen also targeted

Sunnis who had lived with Shia in the south for centuries.
Under the loose tutelage of the Ottomans, the Al Saadun, a
Sunni tribe originating from the Arabian Peninsula, had led a
confederation of predominantly Shia tribes, the Muntafiq, and
defended Shia against the warrior monks of Muhammad ibn
Abd al-Wahhab who raided Najaf and Karbala in 1802. "Religion
cannot be brought by the sword," the Al Saadun tribal leader was
reputed to have cried. A provincial capital, Nasiriya, was named
after its chieftain, Nasir al-Saadun Pasha, who founded the
town in the late nineteenth century. Under the monarchy, the Al
Saadun kept their elevated status. Saddam Hussein appointed
an Al Saadun his interior minister. King Faisal of Saudi Arabia
made a Saadoun, Abdel Muhsin, his prime minister, and Saddam
Hussein appointed one interior minister. The Iraqi branches of
the Communist Party and the Ba'ath Party, which first emerged
from Nasiriya, began in part as Shia working-class protest
movements against their Sunni overlords.

But the path America's invasion had made for armed exiles
to return from Iran upset the old power structures. Saddam's
apparatchiks fled, and Sunnis who stayed found they faced a
glass ceiling when seeking government jobs. The city's opera
house, where divas had sung arias in the 1950s, was converted
into a hall for performing the *lutm*, the chest-beating dirge that
accompanies Shia memorials. Shia chauvinists dubbed Sunnis a
fifth column, and as the latter's alienation intensified, the label
became self-fulfilling. Dozens were incarcerated on suspicion
of repeated attacks on Nasiriya's high-security Hout prison,
where under arc lights America jailed the highest-risk al-Qaeda
and Ba'ath Party leaders, including Saddam's foreign minister

120   Tariq Aziz, who died there in June 2015. In 2012 the suicide
bombing of a pilgrimage procession at the gates to the town
triggered the first pogrom. Police found it easier to scapegoat
the Al Saadun clan than catch the culprit. Apparently fearing his
own assassination at the hands of Shia militiamen if his ruling
was not to their liking, a circuit judge sentenced 13 Sunnis to life
imprisonment and one to death.

Most of Nasiriya's Sunnis have now left Iraq and headed back
to Saudi Arabia, from whence, several centuries ago, they came.
The few who remain receive death threats slipped under their
doors. When I went to meet a Sunni family who lived on a date
plantation across the river, a visiting Shia businessman demanded
my passport and called the local intelligence chief. My taxi driver,
who turned out to have been a local policeman, shook with fear. I
finally found someone who admitted to being of Al Saadun stock
on a farm out of town. "You're not wanted," read a piece of hate mail
he recently received. "Leave." When he talks of Nasiriya's Sunnis,
he uses the past tense. "There were Jews here once, too," he says.

In the far south, Basra's Sunnis have hung on for longer. In 2003,
they comprised perhaps 15 percent of the population and the
core of the mercantile elite of a province so awash with oil it
provides 95 percent of the government's oil revenues. But the
killing of clerics, the burning of mosques, and attacks on Sunni
officials have also depleted their ranks. Mass rural migration
from poor Shia provinces into squalid shantytowns that ring the
city has only exacerbated the decline of the Sunni share of the
population and the sense of siege that they feel. The religious
parties ruling Basra use their grip on the governorate's budget

to control university appointments, and award tenure according to party allegiance. Basra's five cinemas remain shuttered 12 years after the American invasion. The restaurants on the banks of the Shatt al-Arab have reopened, but not the bars that once attracted thousands of pleasure-seekers from the dry Gulf. "The last bar till Bahrain," bemoans a boozer in a Baghdad bar, Jannat al-Ahlam. Attempts to offer an alternative vision are shot down. In the 2013 local elections, only one Sunni was elected to Basra's 23-man council. Two Sunni councilors elected in the neighboring town of Az Zubayr were both killed. A Sunni elder played me footage recorded by security cameras of uniformed police officers hauling an oil ministry official in late 2014 into an unregistered white van as he walked through a Basra market.

For a time Az Zubayr had been a byword for southern Sunni resistance. Its people lived up to their namesake. Az Zubayr ibn Al-Awam was one of the early Sunni commanders who fought Islam's first civil war against Imam Ali at the Battle of the Camel in Basra. In the nineteenth century, the town had been a refuge for Sunni tribes that spilled out of Najd fleeing the northern advance of the Al Sauds. And after Saddam Hussein launched his faith campaign in the 1990s, its mosques were a first stop for Saudi Salafis gravitating to Iraq. After 2003, America and Britain incarcerated many of Sunni inhabitants, including the local Al Saadun chief, in Camp Bucca, triggering the first wave of suicide bombings. But a decade later, Zubair's Sunni elders seem broken. The Sunni share of the town's population had fallen from 90 percent to 10 percent, Sheikh Jamal al-Dosari, the imam of its main Sunni mosque told me. Of the town's 40 Sunni mosques, only 15 open for Friday prayers. "Basra was known as Iraq's most cosmopolitan city," says Ramzi Mostaf, a Kurd who had spent his life in Basra as a civil servant in the higher education ministry. When a row erupted between Shia and Kurdish politicians in Baghdad, he fled after receiving death-threats.

All told, the south of Iraq is becoming almost as single-sect as its north. In tandem with the flight of Sunnis, its non-Muslim population has fallen to marginal levels. Until Saddam Hussein's fall, 400 Christian families lived in Amarah, another provincial city on the southern reaches of the Tigris. When I visited in October 2015, just 12 remained. "Four families left three weeks ago," bemoaned their community leader, insisting he would be last to leave. Mandeans, the biblical-era Baptists, tell a similar tale. From 50,000 in Basra in 2000, they numbered just 4,000 in 2015. Those too, says Basra's Mandean community leader, Emad Awra, are preparing to leave. "Why don't you wear the veil and become Muslim?" his daughter had been asked in front of her all-Muslim class. The headmaster had assured him it would not happen again. He wasn't sure.

Haider al-Abadi

Saddam Hussein's cavernous Republican palace seems several sizes too big for the man tasked with turning a country ruled by sectarian militias into a state. Saddam filled it with his megalomania; America with its occupying army of soldiers, spies, and carpetbaggers. On the way to Prime Minister Haider al-Abadi's antechamber, I passed the locked offices of Paul Bremer, the American governor who gutted the state and laid the foundations of its current dysfunction. Al-Abadi, who is a jolly man, was reminiscing about his modest home in Karrada, a central Baghdad neighborhood, with its small garden where he would sit sipping lemon and mint tea, klaxons hooting in the background. "I'd had it renovated and was moving back in," he says forlornly. "And then they made me prime minister."

At any time, he would have made an unusual Middle East leader. In the grip of a war on the Islamic State, his appointment in August 2014 as prime minister and head of the armed forces seemed almost obtuse. He had not held any military post, and in his youth he dodged the draft.

Initially, Abadi's popularity ratings climbed, particularly among Sunnis, who welcomed his inclusive messaging, his occasional visits to their mosques, and—in marked contrast to his predecessor—his aversion to bellicose threats. The problem was his ability to deliver.

On his Facebook page, he promised to open the Green Zone, the forbidden city the Americans carved out of central Baghdad in 2003 whose closure had bunged up the capital ever since. But all that transpired was a sole one-way road, disrupted by so many checkpoints that the old traffic jams seemed more bearable. He abolished the three vice presidents under him, and gave them and their hundreds of security guards 48 hours to leave their official residences, but did nothing when the deadline expired. "Under the constitution, he doesn't have the jurisdiction," protested one of them, Ayad Allawi. "These are not reforms, they are hostile measures." To prune expenditures he proposed halving the $25,000 monthly allowance MPs receive for their security details; Parliament overruled him, citing the principle of its sovereignty.

124   He did little to hide the constraints he felt on his exercise
of power. As a member of the Islamic Dawa Party, he owes his
job to the political system, but remains a bit player in it. Party
apparatchiks address his predecessor, Nouri al-Maliki, and not
him, as al-Zaim, the leader. The factions divvy up government
posts and appoint his cabinet. "If he'd have touched the party
system, we'd probably have shot him," says a middle-ranking
Dawa hand.

The most immediate threat to the prime minister's tenure came less from the jihadis over the horizon than the Shia
warlords of the *hashad* sharing his Green Zone. Courteously,
al-Abadi praises the *hashad* for rolling IS back from Baghdad's
gates. It succeeded, he says, in puncturing the psychological
pall that IS had cast over Iraq, and for the first time forced IS
onto the defensive. But he admits, too, that the *hashad*'s victories might have proven a double-edged sword. "Any force that
you arm is a threat," he tells me, sounding more like a pundit
than Iraq's chief decision-maker. "I remember in some countries with a history of *coups d'etat*, usually leaders are afraid of
arming the army. And the same I think [holds] for this popular
mobilization force." He spoke of plans to incorporate Sunnis
into the *hashad* and assign all territories the *hashad* liberates
to local police forces. When I suggest that he might lack the
capacity to deliver, he agrees, and voices concern at commanders nursing "uncontrollable vendettas." The number of
soldiers that loyalists have under their command "is very few."

"How will Iraq disarm the *hashad*?" asks Wathiq al-
Hashami, a political scientist at Baghdad University. Mowaffak
al-Rubaie, al-Maliki's former national security advisor, shares

the concern. The *hashad*, he says, "saved the day for Baghdad,
but could yet destroy Iraq." Buoyed by their popular standing,
militia commanders, he ventures, might march on Baghdad.

Few Iraqis in the south openly champion separation. In a meeting
with four professors at the University of Kufa's engineering
department, three of them waxed lyrical about the golden age
that awaits a united Iraq, or at least its Arab provinces, once the
hashad vanquishes IS. But a dissenting fourth engineer quietly
questioned why the south should bother. As long as Sistani's
jihad defended Shias from IS's predations he supported it, but
why shed blood for a Sunni population that is neither welcoming
nor particularly wanted, he asked. The further north the militia
advances, the more lives are lost, and the returns from the battle
diminish. Compared to the south's mineral wealth, the Sunni
provinces offer few natural resources. Much of it is desert, and
its feuding tribes will only cause trouble. Better, he argued, to
safeguard what the south already has. In short, he said, breaking
a taboo by uttering a word he claims many privately espouse,
why not opt for *taqsim*—partition. A heavy silence followed.

Modern
Milleticide

Part Five

The Spread of Sunni Revanchism

In his consciously Spartan office on a backstreet of Abu Dhabi, the United Arab Emirates' capital, Mohammed Dahlan feigns the air of a man who has retired from the tribulations of public office. His teeth are hurting, and his next appointment is with the dentist.

"I'm no longer the young guard," he sighs like a pensioner. "It's time for a younger generation. I've finished with my ego." Much of the meeting is consumed with a nostalgic roll call of the regional and international powerbrokers he has supped with.

For all the pretense of a has-been, Dahlan is 52, and looks a decade younger. He wears a boyish blue T-shirt and spends three hours each day in the gym. Born in a Gaza refugee camp, he has bruised and charmed his way out of the squalor of Israel's occupation, and climbed to the highest echelons of the Middle East's politics. For decades he led Palestine's preventative security force, until, equally threatened by the strongman, Hamas's rulers

128   in Gaza and Palestine's president Mahmoud Abbas in the West
Bank found rare agreement and chased him from their respective
realms in 2007. Exiled in Abu Dhabi, he exuded the air of a man
who had outgrown his homeland and aspired to a regional role. He
advises a brash younger generation of Emirati princes who flash
the power and enormous wealth their more discreet father, Sheikh
Zayed, preferred not to flaunt. Mohammed bin Zayed Al Nahyan,
the UAE's crown prince and de facto ruler, made him his security
advisor and tasked him with projecting his economic, political,
and military reach. One day Dahlan is in Belgrade buying up Air
Serbia, which flies to Israel, the next in Libya's Green Mountains
helping General Khalifa Haftar, another sometime interlocutor
with the CIA, restructure his security apparatus.

        When we met in early 2015, Dahlan's latest preoccupation
was Yemen. The UAE was committing 100 fighter jets to help
Mohammed bin Salman, the Saudi defense minister and 29-year-
old son of the king, stand up to Yemen's first Sunni leader, Abd
Rabbuh Mansur Hadi, on the country's predominantly Shia
population. Unlike Iraq's mainstream Shia, Yemen's stemmed
from the Zaidiyyah, a splinter sect that had historically
maintained good ties with Sunnis. In the 1960s they had allied
with Saudi Arabia, forming a royalist front against Gamal Abdel
Nasser's republican forces. They shared only the first four imams
with mainstream Shiism, and like Sunnis did not deem their
leaders to be infallible.

        Such theological subtleties were lost on the Gulf's young
leaders, who were determined to reverse what they saw as the
comatose and reactive policies enacted by the conservative
gerontocracy they inherited. Owing to the passivity of their
fathers, three Arab capitals had fallen to Iranian influence,

as they saw it—Damascus, Beirut, and Baghdad. They were determined not to lose a fourth, Sana'a. "More than a billion Sunnis have simply had enough of them," said a former director general of the Saudi Intelligence Agency, Prince Bandar bin Sultan, referring to Shia generally.

Tasked with helping to implement the crown prince's policies, Dahlan's strategy was to light multiple fires across the region and hope to draw in and then burn Iran. In an attempt to bankrupt a republic just as it was emerging from sanctions, he said, Gulf states had opened the spigots so wide that the oil price would collapse by three-quarters. To counter Iran's own Shia proxies, he said, Saudi Arabia was sponsoring Sunni militias, deploying the same a policy of spreading jihad abroad that it had previously used in Afghanistan. Qatar, the UAE, and Turkey all joined Saudi Arabia in arming Syria's "rebelution" aimed at replacing the Assad regime with Sunni rule. While Saudi Arabia financed the Islamic Front, Qatar and Turkey supplied the al-Nusra Front, an al-Qaeda offshoot. In addition to guns, they gave preachers airtime on their copious satellite channels, who used sectarian diatribes to rally recruits. Yemen was Dahlan's latest test case. Maintaining its Shia satellites, from Lebanon's Hezbollah to Yemen's Houthis, would cost Iran $30 billion annually, said Dahlan. "We have to suck them in," he said.

Under the baton of the Gulf states a pan-Sunni front was coalescing. Mohammed bin Salman, the acting regent of Saudi Arabia, sought to close fractious Sunni ranks and made overtures to the more pliable branches of the Muslim Brotherhood. Recep Tayyip Erdoğan, Turkey's hitherto estranged president, paid a rare visit to Riyadh and denounced Iran's "hegemonic" ambitions. With an eye to maintaining Gulf funding, Egypt's

130   president, Abdel Fattah el-Sisi, declared that the battle had
begun for the region's identity. In place of proxy militias, they
spoke of assembling a conventional Sunni army and girding it
for battle. Gulf states redirected their planes from supporting
the American bombing of IS to targeting Yemen. Sunni fighters
from Senegal and Sudan all signed up to fight the Houthis, and
after some hesitation Pakistan declared its readiness to defend
Saudi borders. With a disregard for world heritage that shared
much with IS's outlook, not to speak of their own leveling of
Mecca's shrines, fighter jets flattened several of the caked-mud
medieval high-rises in Sana'a's Old City that gave it the look of
a gingerbread land. Within weeks of ascending his throne, King
Salman and his young son had set the stage for a Sunni-on-Shia
showdown.

For almost a thousand years, the Zaidiyyah had ruled in isolation
to the rest of the Shia world. War blurred such nuances. Fellow
Shias, all too silent when Bashar al-Assad's forces dropped barrel
bombs, voiced outrage at the Saudi-led aerial bombing. "The
Arabs are conspiring," read the headline on the front page of a
Shia-owned newspaper in Baghdad, *al-Mustaqbal al-Iraqi* , after
the Arab League approved Saudi Arabia's plans for a Sunni army.
Kuwait's Shia parliamentarians released a rare denunciation
of Saudi "aggression." Saudi Arabia's Shias—Ismailis in the
southwest, mainstream Shia in the Eastern Province, and
the very large number of Yemeni migrants—judiciously held
their silence, but declined to endorse the Al Sauds' war. Bahrain's
suppressed Shia majority who had waged an intermittent
intifada against a despotic Sunni monarchy, wondered whether
Shias elsewhere might finally come to their rescue.

For eight years, from 1980 to 1988, Arab Shias fought Persian Shias in a struggle to define national borders. A generation on, confessional loyalties had supplanted national ones. Freed from Saddam's clutches and with IS pushed out of range, millions of pilgrims from Shia communities worldwide converged on Iraq's holy sites for the Arba'een, the annual commemoration of the massacre of the Prophet's grandsons, Hasan and Husayn, whom Shia venerate as their second and third imams. (Unlike Saudi Arabia's haj, there were remarkably few casualties caused by mismanagement). Encouraged by Iran, militias were on the move, too, taking the place of depleted and demoralized national armies. Hazaras from Afghanistan joined Hezbollah fighters from Lebanon in bolstering Assad's beleaguered regime against a predominantly rural Sunni revolt. Alawites formed their own shields, or militias, and the Houthis established Ansar Allah, modelled on Hezbollah, which pushed south to the gates of Aden. The Badr Organization's training camp in Al-Jadriya, one of Baghdad's plushest neighborhoods, sent excess Iraqi volunteers from the oversubscribed *hashad* as well. Portraits of Iraqi fighters who had died defending the Shia complex at Sayyidah Zaynab Mosque in Damascus hung from the steel rafters in the camp. At a memorial in honor of the Iraqi fighters killed in Syria, nine-year-old orphans in military fatigues stood stoically to attention as the crowds chanted "Hussein."

Professors and politicians participating in debates at the weekly Friday bookfair on Baghdad's Mutanabbi Street posited matching Saudi Arabia's proposed Sunni army with a Shia one. Some wondered whether it already existed, as Iran's once clandestine military presence in the Arab world shed its camouflage. From Syria to Yemen, General Qasem Soleimani, the commander of the al-Quds Brigades, a division of the Revolutionary Guards that functioned as Iran's foreign legion, publicly inspected militia front lines. In 2003, King Abdullah of Jordan had warned of a Shia crescent extending from the western borders of Afghanistan to the Mediterranean. With forces in Iran, Iraq, and Yemen encircling the Sunni Gulf states, that arc was beginning to resemble a full moon.

The Al Khalifas, the ruling family of Bahrain, had long prided themselves on their islands' pluralism. In response to the critics who berated their intransigent monopoly of power and discrimination against their indigenous Shia, they pointed to the profusion of Hindu temples, Jewish synagogues, and Muslim Brotherhood associations that other Gulf monarchies banned."They never touched our *hussainias*,"—congregation halls—said a Shia leader from the village of Bani Jamra. But when in February 2011, after the fall of Tunisia's and Egypt's autocrats, Sunnis and Shias staged mass demonstrations on Pearl Roundabout in Manama, the capital, to call for democracy and a share of power, the Al Khalifas fanned sectarian sentiments to divide the protesters' ranks. Driving across the 16-kilometer causeway that joined the two kingdoms, the Saudis brought not only their tanks but their creed. Within weeks the security forces demolished some 60 Shia *hussainias*. When I visited in May 2011, scavengers were still picking through their remains.

Of all the Arab Spring protests of 2011, that against Bahrain's Sunni monarchy had been the most civil. Unlike the islands' *initifada* in the mid-1990s, the protesters refrained from burning tires and shunned sectarian polemic. By casting their opponents as Shia revolutionaries bent on subjugation of the Sunni minority, the Al Khalifas elevated themselves into defenders of the faith. Anti-Shia measures intensified. Princes and officers patronized the mosque of Jassim Al Saeedi, the island's leading Salafi preacher, who demanded the expulsion of Bahrain's Shias. When Al Saeedi stood as a candidate in the West Riffa constituency, home to the king and his coterie of army officers, he won. Local oilmen and doctors with Shia origins lost their jobs; foreign workers from Arab Sunni states took their place. "We won," said Mona, an Egyptian clerk in Gulf Air's head office, celebrating her promotion with a round of whiskey sours in a Manama pub. Across the region, sect had become a secular rather than religious badge of identity. Though religious leaders damned them both, Saudi male prostitutes were said to spurn Shia clients in gay chatrooms.

Communal life in Bahrain's few remaining mixed towns crumbled under the weight of the polarization. Hamad Town, a purpose-built commuter-ville, had been an experiment in inter-faith living. Some 50,000 middle-class Sunnis and Shias shared its housing blocs, shops, and schools. Inter-marriage was common. But as tensions grew, Sunnis and Shias gravitated to separate cafés. A Facebook page listed the Shia commercial establishments Sunnis should boycott. With woeful ill timing, Tehran Grills, a Persian restaurant, opened in January 2011. Next door, Jasmis, a fast-food outlet, distributed free meals to Sunni gangs who preyed on protesters attempting to march on King Hamad's palace. A Sunni preacher established a network of Sunni-run markets to break what he called "the Shia monopoly on our food supply." Some Shia shops were smashed, and fighting erupted between Sunnis and Shias in the local girls' school and on the University of Bahrain's campus nearby. "We still say hello to

134 Shia neighbors," says an off-duty policewoman who decorated her Chevrolet Estate with a Saudi flag. "But we don't trust them like before. If they'd have won, they would have given Bahrain to Iran."

Though Shia protesters were beaten back from the main roads, their villages running along Bahrain's northern coast survive as radicalized enclaves. By day, residents go to work in the private businesses that still employ them; by night, they gather in squares seething with rebellion. On stages made of pallets masked actors enact passion spiels depicting the Sunni tyrants who through the ages have killed their imams. Actvists hand out leaflets calling for toppling the king. Billboards are filled with faces of babies the authorities are said to have asphyxiated with tear gas. "Death to Hamad," reads the graffiti on the walls. Doctors expelled from government hospitals run makeshift clinics treating protesters wounded when hurling petrol bombs at the tanks and armored cars patrolling the highway that runs past their villages. And on holidays, Shia villagers briefly reclaim Manama, the capital, with religious processions. "We commemorate the most minor festivals— even more than Iran," says a former parliamentarian as we stand watching a parade of bare-breasted chest-thumping men march through the city center to mark the killing of Ali ibn Husayn, a great-grandson of the Prophet, in the eighth century. Volunteers hand out free sweetmeats and sweet sheep milk. Tableaux of Shia saints hang from rooftops. Not a policeman is in sight. *"Hay hat hylhat, minna al-dhila,"* they chant (we will not submit), repeating the last cry of the Prophet's grandson Imam Husayn as he opted for martyrdom over submission to his Sunni tormentor, the caliph Yazid.

If the causeway carried Sunni suppression one way, it brought Shia anxiety back. Though located atop the world's most bountiful oil fields, the Shia towns in Saudi Arabia's Eastern Province are among the kingdom's least developed. In the first weeks of the Arab Spring, Shias in the towns of Al-Awamiyah and Qatif marched in unison with their counterparts in Bahrain, staging rallies to protest the institutional discrimination and anti-Shia derision many Saudis take for granted. Even in Shia areas, school textbooks term Shia *rafida*, or rejectionists, and Sunni teachers chide pupils who celebrate Shia rites as *kuffar*. And though countrywide Shias comprise some 10 percent of the population, the king has yet to appoint a Shia cabinet minister.

The protests were easily quelled. The security forces opened fire. On New Year's Day 2016, Nimr Baqir al-Nimr, a Shia ayatollah who had led the protests, was executed for sedition. But increasingly, its population looked for alternative sources of defense to the state. When IS's suicide bombers blew up packed husseiniyas on three successive Friday prayers in 2015, social media from Qatif lampooned the Saudi authorities, not only for failing to protect them but for disseminating the anti-Shia ideology that inspired the attacks. Some began organizing their own embryonic hashad to secure their mosques. The Saudis increased their heavily-protected checkpoints around Qatif, as much to tighten their hold on a restive Shia population as to deter fresh attacks. As the sectarian battles flared across the region, Grand Ayatollah Sistani's representative declared that for the first time since Saddam's overthrow, he would not be sending a representative on haj to Mecca.

Communal Rupture

From the ashes of war, a new geopolitical map is emerging. From Aden to Anbar, the last multi-confessional vestiges of the Ottoman Empire are transmuting into a patchwork of little irredentist entities, which in some ways make Israel feel rather at home.

To keep out the influx of Arab Iraqi refugees, the Kurds erected a 2.5-meter high barricade replete with deep trenches like a Maginot Line along the southern frontier of their Kurdistan Regional Government. Arab Iraqis arriving by air received a one-week travel visa, lest they turn Kurdistan once again into a polyglot land. Over-stayers were warned on their mobile phones of the fines they risked if they failed to depart. The area traded its own oil and gas, sometimes with Israel, and American forces conducted joint operations with Kurdish *pesh-merga* forces, sometimes bypassing the authorities in Baghdad.

In Syria, the Assad regime's power increasingly retrenched into its Alawite base. Sunni rebel-held areas reopened informal supply lines with the Arabian Peninsula, reinforcing ties fostered by generations of inter-marriage between the Shammar and Azeza Bedouin tribes straddling the Saudi border. In the Orontes Valley, the mixed cities of Hama and Homs nervously watched as mortar fire tore apart their multi-faith world

From its two cities of Raqqa and Mosul, IS's caliphate, too, acquired staying power, erasing old frontiers to create a new entity holding sway over a third of Syria and a third of Iraq. Despite more than a year of American-led coalition bombing and some 11,000 airstrikes by October 2015, IS remained amongst the more economically stable parts of the region. Much like an earlier manifestation of Salafi rule, that of the Al Sauds' in Nejd, they protected the roads in their territory from marauding tribesmen and stamped out extortion. Christians who remained paid the *jizya* in exchange for basic protection. The sale of oil, IS's main source of income, netted revenues of over $500 million a year. A year of bombardment was estimated to have killed some 15,000 IS fighters, but their numbers had been more than replenished by a continued influx from abroad and the introduction of conscription within, furnishing IS with a combined force of between 70,000 and 100,000 men.

The urban middle class who still had the means to pay people-smugglers fled to Europe, emptying the region of the educated, cosmopolitan constituency that despaired of ever again recovering the pluralism in which they had been raised. Christians and minorities received preferential treatment, but Muslims too found copious back routes into Europe. They could be found huddled in the basement car parks of tourist resorts of southwestern Turkey, waiting their turn for passage to the Greek islands. A daytrip cost Europeans $17. They paid smugglers $800 a head. The risks were great—more than 3,000 drowned in the Mediterranean in 2015. Some spoke of babies thrown overboard to stop their crying when Greece's coast guard patrols approached to escape detection; others of smugglers who fleeced their passengers before abandoning boat.

But the risks of staying were greater. The region they left behind was unrecognizable, dominated by rural warlords who had captured the cities and used the schools for shelter. Those stuck in the squalor of Jordan's and Syria's camps found scant respite. Banned from work, refugees had to choose between seeing their daughters prostitute themselves or returning home to IS for the $100 it paid its fighters a month.

A century earlier, the collapse of the Ottoman order had prompted seven million Turks to flee Europe, and cast millions more Christians out of Anatolia. The collapse of Middle Eastern nation-states was propelling even larger numbers on the move. In similar ways to the western flank of the former Ottoman Empire two decades earlier, the eastern flank was Balkanizing. In place of the ideal of the nationstate, a mosaic of xenophobic, chauvinistic, self-obsessed sects ruled patches of land whose frontiers had been gerrymandered to give minorities a semblance of majority rule.

But whereas the Balkans had the advantage of membership to an umbrella organization, the European Union, to dilute tensions, the Middle East's confessional states have no broader common institution to appeal to. Bereft of an over-arching structure, the new confessional entities seem set to fortify their defenses, clamor for the defense of whatever minorities remained beyond their borders, and collide along the new fault lines. The latest attempt to reorganize the Ottoman Empire looks set to be no more harmonious than the last.

Holy Lands to Holy Communities

Part Six

The Way Back:
An Armenian
Perspective

At times, Ara Sarafian, an exiled Armenian historian, could be something of a Jeremiah. "They might as well have danced on their graves," he sulked, when he caught the descendants of the victims and perpetrators of the Armenian genocide dancing together on the centennial of the slaughter. For a week, he had led a mix of Turks, Kurds, Assyrian Christians, and Armenians on a pilgrimage through Anatolia—or, as he called it, Western Armenia—mapping the communities annihilated 100 years earlier. On the dry riverbed where Turkish soldiers handed over shackled Armenians to Kurdish tribesmen to dispose of, he lectured on the possibilities of reconciliation, once Turkey acknowledged the past. On the green hillside above, an elderly Kurd sung dirges for the dead. Turkish participants gathered poppies and forget-me-nots that grew in the killing fields and handed them to Armenians. On the road back to their hotel his exhausted party fell asleep

142 on each other's shoulders. But dancing together on such a sober occasion seemed altogether a little too glib.

It had been a difficult week. To avoid global hectoring, Turkish president Recep Tayyip Erdoğan had cynically shifted the victory celebrations for the Gallipoli Campaign, the battle where Ottoman forces repelled an Allied invasion a century earlier, to coincide with the centennial of the Armenian genocide. Armenian ministers had upped the ante, demanding that Turkey restore the vast tracts of land they took from them. "They want confrontation," said Sarafian of Armenian officials. "They want to destabilize Turkey by demanding territory. They want Turkey to implode." Far from coming to terms with the past, officials on both sides regurgitated tired historical narratives and manipulated historical memories to pick at old wounds.

Sarafian, by contrast, was on a mission to recover the regional pluralism that Armenia's genocide had unpicked. Sometimes, like the bones of the mass graves he exposed, the values lay surprisingly close to the surface. At 3 p.m. on April 24, 2015, Genocide Remembrance Day, he began marching to St. Sarkis, an Armenian church in the southeastern city of Diyarbakır, which had been wrecked in the genocide and was now given over to weeds.

When he set off from the city's old black basalt walls, there were more riot police than mourners. But with each step the numbers grew. By the time Sarafian reached the church, hundreds of townsfolk marched in solidarity to commemorate the anniversary. Many wore T-shirts printed in Armenia's national color, purple, some inscribed with the words *Beni Unutma* (Armenian for never forget). And amidst the ruins, one politician after another took to a makeshift stage to declare their contrition for their complicity in the killing. "How can we look Armenians in the eye?" asked Gültan Kışanak, Diyarbakır's co-mayor. "We share a collective shame." None of the speakers in a town considered a bastion of Kurdish nationalism offered the excuse of wartime, which might have mitigated the crime, or recalled the "righteous Kurds" who had rescued Armenians and had their homes burned as a result. "To deny the genocide is to commit the genocide afresh," said Selahattin Demirtaş, a former presidential candidate and leader of Turkey's main pro-Kurdish party, the Peoples' Democratic Party.

In the process of exposing the past, many of Turkey's Kurds are discovering Armenian roots. I have an Armenian grandmother, Kurds used to say, innocently sidestepping the details of how she was acquired; more commonly today they describe themselves as part Armenian and acknowledge the less savory reality. Many Kurds "rescued" Armenian children from the death marches and took them as slave girls and concubines.

Perhaps remorse is easier for Kurds than for Ankara's leaders. The Kurds were the lowly implementing agents, not the masterminds. As fellow victims of Turkish nationalism, they can also empathize with Armenian pain. After breakfasting on Christians, a Kurdish lawyer in Diyarbakır told me, Turks lunched on Kurds. Three generations after eliminating Armenians, who once comprised a third of Eastern Anatolia's population, Turkish nationalists torched 3,000 Kurdish villages in the 1980s. In both the intent was the same: to eradicate difference and impose a uniform identity.

A more cynical analyst might have deconstructed the event as a Kurdish political ploy to foment anti-Turkish sentiment.

144   Sarafian, who has a knack for delivering dramatic sentences in a disarmingly deadpan expression, saw it as an act of "catharsis." A growing caucus across Turkey, he said, was struggling to overcome sectarian and ethnic chauvinism and restore the kinship Turks, Armenians, Kurds, and Assyrians once shared. "I don't want to sever my Turkish connections," he said. "I want a country that gives Armenians the choice to live here not as foreigners but as people with a special status who belong here."

As Sarafian sees it, such a policy shift would constitute a vital guarantor of stability. "Ottoman values" would equip Turkey with the flexibility to accommodate its disparate identities, and transform an unstable monoculture into a sustainable melting pot. Sarafian argues that only Ottomanism, underpinned by democracy, would ensure Turkey's survival as a modern state.

When Sarafian first arrived in Turkey in the 1980s, the country was emerging from military rule. Diyarbakır remained under de facto military occupation. Even whispers in Kurdish were banned, and he was expelled for photographing a ruined church. Thirty years on, Turkey was again a polyglot society. The country has all but legalized Kurdish, and despite the flare-up of fighting in Diyarbakir at the time of writing, the country had licensed Kurdish political parties. For two successive elections in 2015, the Peoples' Democratic Party surpassed the 10 percent threshold designed to prevent it entering parliament.

For the first time since the abolition of the caliphate in 1924, Turkey has permitted the construction of a new church in 2015. Near the Greek border at Edirne, it has restored and reopened the city's imposing synagogue. Turkish universities

puncture taboos by hosting conferences exploring the Young
Turks' expulsion of Greeks—in tandem, of course, with studies
of the Greek expulsion of Turks.

Turkey's recovery of pluralism remains far from guaranteed.
Erdoğan has called for the restoration of church property, but
has authorized the reopening of only a handful of the thousands
of churches whose bells once pealed across Anatolia. He entered
into peace talks with the banned Kurdistan Workers' Party,
and then resumed fighting. The appeal to a pluralist past often
seems little more than a political tool by Erdoğan and his fellow
Islamist politicians to overturn Kemalism, whose anti-religious
zeal smothered Islam almost as comprehensively as other
faiths. In his embrace of Ottomanism detractors and supporters
alike detect a covert ambition to convert his presidency into a
caliphate.

Yet even on the issue of genocide, observers sense the government is shifting. After four generations of indoctrination
and governments that refused even to debate the matter, ministers now accept the suffering but argue over the degree. Some
500,000 Armenians had died of hunger and disease in a forcible relocation to the Syrian Desert, argued a senior official, but
the deportations were justified on the grounds that Armenian
revolutionaries were helping Russian forces invade. Deputy
Prime Minister Bülent Arınç spoke of "an unintentional genocide"; Prime Minister Ahmet Davutoğlu called it "a tragedy of
innocents." Though Erdoğan escaped to Gallipoli on the centennial, he sent a minister to the Armenian Orthodox Church's
commemoration in his stead, and the speech given in Erdoğan's
name publicly offered his condolences. The country's leading

146   newspapers gave more coverage to the genocide's centennial than Gallipoli's. "Never again," declared *Cumhuriyet* across its front page in heavy black font—in Armenian as well as Turkish.

Armenian nationalists take little comfort from Erdoğan, and many survivors and their scattered descendants refuse to engage until Turkey admits culpability for a genocide that killed 1.5 million of their kin—intentionally, not as a regrettable side effect of war. But across Eastern Anatolia local mayors solicit Sarafian's help in encouraging Armenians and Assyrian Christians to visit their lost homeland. Assyrian Christians from Australia came with apps on their mobile phones mapping their churches that had once dotted Diyarbakır. Some discuss the prospects of a proper return and ask about applying for Turkish citizenship on the basis of their ancestors' Ottoman citizenship. A French Armenian lawyer even lodged a case in the Turkish courts seeking the return of the land on which Batman Airport was built. "Politically," says Sarafian, "the shift has already happened."

We were standing by the Monument of Common Conscience, a temporary sculpture Diyarbakır's Kurdish-led municipality had erected two years earlier at the base of the Old City's walls. Beneath a tear drop was an inscription in Turkish, Kurdish, English, Armenian, Syriac, Hebrew, and Zaza, promising an end to religious and ethnic persecution. Sarafian was still brooding about the dance of the descendants of soldier, executioner, and victim the night before. Perhaps, he retracted, it might have been the right way to commemorate: "We don't want to divorce," he said. "We want to reconcile."

The Way Back:
Shia Perspectives

The refinery on the highway into Baghdad pumps black fumes into the sky as if signaling the entrance to a vast crematorium. Convoys of *hashad*, bound for the front, weave through rush-hour traffic, testing their guns. Barricaded by iron gates, residential compounds resemble prison camps. America's most visible legacy in Baghdad, the towering concrete blocs that link to form fortified walls, scar the cityscape like industrial weeds.

Yet once inside this fortified shell, signs of budding normalization begin to surface. New overpasses span clogged intersections. A sleek Chinese train pulls out of the Baghdad's grand railway station—built to the same model as the majestic Viceroy's House in Delhi—bound for Basra, cutting the journey time to an almost bearable ten hours. Cranes haul the last glass panels onto a skyscraper sporting an office bloc, large mall, and five-story hotel. Suicide bombs, which once peaked

148 at 17 a day, have fallen to perhaps one a week, Prime Minister Haider al-Abadi proudly notes. Although Baghdad has as many checkpoints as most cities have traffic lights, the only time I heard gunfire was when that *hashad* convoy drove past. "We have yet to hear a mortar this year," a Western diplomat in the Green Zone told me.

For the first time in decades, the country, too, has a leader with no militia or guard to his name. Al-Abadi is a rarity in the region—a leader who has come from neither a dynasty nor an army. Perhaps the militias and foreign powers wanted a weak and malleable incumbent, but when he challenged their remit, the public, tired of the militias and their sectarianism that have torn the country apart, rallied en masse in his support in cities across southern Iraq. His persona alone conjures up a presectarian past. Karrada, al-Abadi's Baghdad neighborhood, had been home to Jews, Christians, and many Sunnis, and though almost entirely Shia today it still retains a bourgeois cosmopolitan air. Artists, musicians, and authors fill its cafés, reviving a civil society suppressed since the 1970s. A frustrated Western diplomat trying to whip up the war effort against IS, whose front lines lie an hour's drive away, likened the atmosphere to the *joie de vivre* that marked Paris under Nazi rule—Iraqis, he complained, have long since learned to suppress their traumas. IS feels more threatening in European capitals than it does in Baghdad. Almost complacently, its inhabitants refer to IS in the past tense. Young men drive through the streets playing pop music that mocks IS's "feminine" fighters at full volume.

Socialites say they have not felt so at ease since the 1970s. A splurge of hip eateries has opened around the University of

Baghdad, where dressed-up girls go to smoke water pipes. Cafés spill onto sidewalks, their tables filled with families late into the night. Closed by Saddam Hussein's faith campaign in the early 1990s, the bars that only tentatively reopened in 2010 are now packed. A banner over the entrance of a nightclub advertises the unveiled starlets who dance on Thursday nights until dawn.

Rather than head to the mosque for midday prayers the following day, thousands throng to Baghdad's old book market on Mutanabbi Street. So crammed were the approach roads that I eventually abandoned my taxi and caught a boat up the Tigris. Undeterred by previous car bombings, university lecturers, senior civil servants, and politicians gather for a weekly literary festival in a cultural center. A Baghdad Scouts troup performs a play denouncing sectarianism. Students shake buckets collecting money to buy back the Yazidi wives and daughters that IS is said to have sold to the Gulf's brothels. Critics heckle the students for inadvertently financing IS. In the cafés lining the alleyways off to the side, disconsolate guitarists strum in an attempt to rise above the clatter. Never have I returned from a foreign assignment so laden with books from interviewees who had just published. The old adage—"Cairo writes, Beirut prints, Baghdad reads"—rings true again.

When in May 2015 a car bomb killed 16 people in Baghdad, Karim Wasfi, conductor of the Iraqi National Symphony Orchestra, arrived at the scene in his black suit and tie as if dressed for a concert, opened his cello case, and played for a gathering crowd. Baghdad's bombs can still wreck lives, but somehow they no longer seem able to wreck a society. By sheer force of demography, Baghdad has won the identity struggle,

150   and the confidence that results means it no longer has quite the same need to prove itself rigidly Shia.

In Najaf, too, the ayatollahs hosted a book fair.

In an annex of the Imam Ali Holy Shrine, an Egyptian bookseller displayed his collection of works by Karl Marx, Kant, and Spinoza. A bookseller from Baghdad kept watch on a cleric who vetted displays. Whenever the censor approached, he turned over the covers of his collections of Sappho's poetry, which sported disrobed women. Once he passed, the bookseller turned them back out. He tells me that his best-selling book was a new Arabic translation of Richard Dawkins's *The Selfish Gene*, a study in the genetics of evolution. It is, he said, particularly favored by seminarians.

Occupying pride of place near the entrance, Lwiis Saliba, a Lebanese theology professor and self-professed Buddhist, sat by his stall selling translations of the religious texts he published. Within two days of the opening he had sold all 50 copies of his new book, *Toward a Christian-Shia Dialogue*, which had a picture of Jesus on its front cover. Arabic translations of the Bible, Talmudic tractates, and Baha'i texts, banned in neighboring Iran, were all selling fast. When a cleric politely requested he remove such heresies, Saliba replied that if the books went, he would go with them. The cleric idled away. While we talked, turbaned seminarians perused an Arabic text of Jewish law first published in Cairo between the wars. "Ninety percent of the books published about Jews in Arabic are anti-Semitic," Saliba explained. "We wanted believers to write about themselves and express their beliefs."

The Najaf book fair is a remarkable testament not just to the openness the ayatollahs have instituted in their Vatican, but to the pliability of religious creeds. Shias like to claim that their faith has long been more broad-minded than mainstream Islam. Ayatollah Khomeini was an expert in Ibn Arabi, a medieval Sufi mystic who some consider an apostate and whose books have been burned in Saudi Arabia.

The glasnost is a fairly recent development. Historically, Shia Islam was xenophobic, hounded, and defensive—more hostile and suspicious of non-Muslims than Sunni Islam. Muhaqqiq al-Hilli, a thirteenth-century scholar and perhaps the greatest exponent of classical Shiism, not only derided non-Muslims as *kuffar*, but prohibited any contact with them lest they corrupted Muslims. Non-Muslims were banned from Shia holy places and at the dinner table. Only after the 1920 revolution against British rule did Grand Ayatollah Muhsin al-Hakim exercise the legal tool of *ijtihad*, which in Shia Islam allows qualified clerics to derive new legal opinions based on reason, and overturned the millennium-old injunction ostracizing the People of the Book.

The sheikh of the Beni Hasan, a vast tribe extending from the Iranian to the Tunisian borders, had been instrumental in the transformation. In his tribal seat outside Najaf, his grandson, Al-Muthana Hatem al-Hassa received me in the same *diwan* where Ayatollah al-Hakim had ruled in favor of eating with Jews. Several sheep had been slaughtered for the cleric's reception, and when guests were summoned to lunch, al-Hassa's grandfather discreetly led his Jewish guest to an outhouse. "Is Itzhak not also of the People of the Book?" interrupted the

152   ayatollah, and summoned the Jew to eat at his side. (His grandson also slaughtered a sheep for me. Unfortunately, I'm a vegetarian. With a tray of mutton in front of us, he reeled at the insult. "Do non-Muslims now refuse to eat with Shia?" he protested.)

Najaf's twenty-first-century ayatollahs are actively engaged in outreach, even with vegetarians. Sistani's representative in Beirut preaches in churches. Another Najafi ayatollah has opened a *hawza* for women. The Hakims shepherd non-Muslims around the Imam Ali's shrine, even bishops with outsized crucifixes swinging on their chests. In contrast to the Wahhabi warriors who banned the *mahmal*, or musical procession that used to accompany the pilgrimage to Mecca, a large crowd of worshippers congregated around a tour group of Shias from Lucknow as they chanted hypnotic Urdu *qasidas*.

Some clerics have begun partnering with the local university, Kufa, to promote inter-faith studies. When I had last visited its campus, the University of Kufa was a burnt-out shell used as an American base. By 2015, it had a new campus and 22 new faculties, including a medical school and a science wing. Encouraged by a grand ayatollah, the turbaned dean of the Islamic Law Faculty ran an inter-faith program, and met me after his Talmud class. "Man is made of two types—a Muslim like you, or a man like you. So be just," he said, quoting Imam Ali. "God, not man, decides who enters paradise."

Other clerics are preparing to introduce inter-faith studies into the *hawza* itself. Facing the threshold of Imam Ali's shrine, Jawad al-Khoei, the son of a former grand ayatollah and a confidante of Sistani, is constructing an 11-story inter-faith academy, designed to be the center point of the hawza. As he shows me round the building site, he points out the location of seven auditoria, a library for 1.5 million books, and a Turkish bath.

While most of the students will be Shia seminarians, there will be a smattering of non-Muslims as well. Al-Khoei is hiring non-Muslim academics to lecture about their respective faiths. "Yazidis will teach us the Yazidi faith," he says. "Our problem in Iraq is our ignorance and denial of the other. The ayatollahs are resolute in their determination to see equal rights for all." His principle of equality is uncompromising: "If the people elect a Christian as leader, he must lead."

As I entered his office, members of a delegation of Yazidi, Christian, Mandean, and Sunni women from Baghdad were taking their leave to meet a grand ayatollah. That evening I found the women again addressing a packed audience at Najaf's writers union about the difficulties of living as a minority under Muslim rule. Najaf had changed them. "After your welcome today, I don't want to return to Baghdad," a Christian housewife said. "I want to stay here. The lowest of you is worth more than our greatest politician. Your doors are open to all."

While IS erases the past in the north, the south seems absorbed in rediscovering it. Iraq's once vibrant Jewish community has long since left, but the country remains gripped by a strange fascination with their memory. "If they'd have stayed the country would have worked better," lamented an Iraqi aid worker. Local television airs documentaries about Baghdad's lost Jews, based on old footage and telephone interviews with exiles. A Baghdad academic, Saad Salloum, has published a collection of essays depicting interaction in Ottoman times: In the seventeenth century the Ottoman sultan Murad IV counted 10,000 Jewish

154   civil servants on his staff; in the nineteenth century, the president of Baghdad's Jewish community, Saleh Sassoon, was also the city's treasurer; and when the British entered Baghdad in the twentieth century, Jews were the city's largest religious group, comprising 80,000 of its 200,000 residents.

As if to compensate for IS's pillaging in the north, curators across southern Iran are rushing to refurbish and open their museums. The National Museum of Iraq, which Americans failed to protect from looters in 2003, reopened in February 2015 after a $40 million renovation. Nasiriya, a city famed for its step ziggurat of Ur, reopened its antiquities museum a month later for the first time since the 1991 Gulf War.

Convention has it that Sunni-Shia relations are locked in an existential struggle dating back to the first generation of Islam. Fighters, politicians, and televangelists from both sects portray their conflict as an elemental schism coursing through Islam's 1,400 years, from Ali's assassination to Saladin's destruction of the Fatimid caliphate to the battles between the Ottoman and Persian empires for supremacy in Iraq. But for much of their history, sectarian strife was an aberration. The Sunni Abbasid caliphs in Baghdad relied on Shia Buyids to keep order. For 350 years, the Ottoman and Persian Empires upheld the Peace of Amasya of 1555, which demarcated borders and gave Shias free passage to visit their holy places and practice their rites in Ottoman-ruled Iraq. The Muntafiq federation, though led by Sunnis, protected Shia from the ravages of Wahhabi raiders from Arabia.

Even after a decade of sectarian strife, Iraqis never tire of emphasizing how Sunnis and Shias share the same dialects, tribes, Prophet, and love of *masqouf*, the fatty carp Iraqis barbeque on the banks of their two rivers. Statisticians say 26 percent still marry outside their sect. "When I travel abroad, I see Sunnis as fellow countrymen, with the same language," a writer from Najaf tells me. "We frequent the same cafés, we share taxis. Why can't we do that at home?"

At his philosophy class in Najaf's Hindi Mosque, Ezzedin al-Hakim posits that sectarianism is a manmade corruption. "The terms Sunni and Shia were not revealed by God. Religion is made by God, but division made by man," he says. Muqtada al-Sadr, though a firebrand cleric when confronting American troops, has reached out to Sunnis, leading prayers in their mosques.

And the country's leading cleric broadcasts appeals for unity. "Do not say Sunnis are our brothers," cautions Grand Ayatollah Sistani. "Say they are us."

The Way Back: Sunni Perspectives

Beneath the towering temples Dubai has built to materialism, my friend Mansour Malik wore a white *galabiya* and white prayer cap when we met. I had not seen him for 20 years. When I had worked for him at the Islamic Law Chambers in a back-street office near London's Brick Lane, helping Bangladeshis with their immigration appeals, he was a Pakistani lawyer delighting in the flexibility of the sharia. But one day he tired of his practice and left to study at the feet of Ahmad Kaftaro, the late mufti of Damascus and a renowned Sufi. Malik had briefly served as a legal advisor to a senior Saudi prince, before tiring of that too and heading to Medina to spend years mediating in the Prophet's mosque. He had remained clean-shaven, he said, because the notion Islam prescribed a beard was bogus. It came from rulings related to *labas*, or clothing, which are mutable according to time and custom, not *ibadat*,

or worship, which are fixed. God said that you had to polish
your heart, not your appearance.

Where Malik sought the modesty, purity, and simplicity
of the oneness of God, Saudi developers had built a Muslim
Las Vegas in Mecca, tempting pilgrims to pour their life sav-
ings into five-star hotels. They had bulldozed the mosque at
Abwa, where the Prophet stopped to weep at the grave of his
mother. They denied non-Muslims access to Mecca, though
the Prophet had lived there with his Christian and Jewish
wives, Maria, Rayhana, and Safiyya. They banned music,
though women had welcomed the Prophet's arrival centuries
ago by singing and banging their tambourines.

Islam's most gracious and merciful God had been hijacked.
Had the Al Sauds also gained custody of Jerusalem's al-Aqsa
Mosque, the cemeteries on the Mount of Olives would now be
parking lots. Nothing, Malik said, has been more corrosive to Islam
than the billions of dollars invested in replacing a pluralist Islam
with a puritanical, anti-women, anti-Western Salafist brand.

Malik blamed the British. In their hunger to conquer and
carve up the Ottoman Empire, its agents had bribed Arabia's
Bedouin tribes to rebel. In the process they had toppled a
Muslim bureaucracy that appointed Jews and Christians to its
upper echelons, and replaced them with nomads who sought
legitimacy by sanctioning Islam's least tolerant strain. The
collapse of the region into a host of intolerant states bickering
over holy land had merely completed a process the British initiated a century ago.

Beyond the peninsula, for over a century Sunni Islam has
been grappling with its loss of status as the region's traditional

ruling sect. It watched, at times passively, as minorities took power and carved Sunni Islam's heartland into Israel, Lebanon, Syria, and then Iraq, and pressed Sunni Muslims to accept their second-rate status. *Dhimmis* and Sunnis swapped roles. As the Sunni realm shrank, the more ferocious it grew. "If you treat Sunnis as pariahs, this is what you get," said Taha Zangana, a Kurdish minister in Erbil, referring to the emergence of IS. "Sunnis can never accept that they don't have power. If they cannot rule over all of Iraq, they will fight to rule a bit of it."

So much had their power receded that at times the violence seemed a nihilistic, destructive last stand. "O Muslims, Islam was never for a day the religion of peace," insisted al-Baghdadi in a sermon. But most of the seven million Sunnis under his rule felt no better for it. "Sunnis are either refugees or under the yoke of IS," bemoaned a tribal chieftain from Mosul. "And yet we seem unable to change course."

Sometimes, though, even the most seemingly firebrand Sunni preachers can surprise with their pluralist vision. For decades, Yunis al-Astal, the most revered preacher of Hamas, had championed jihad against the Israeli occupier and those who pandered to it from his mosque in Gaza's refugee camp of Khan Younis. As an MP and member of Hamas's parliamentary legislative committee, he advocated the introduction of an Islamic penal code, which included crucifixion. From his pulpit on Hamas's satellite channel, he would call on viewers to pick up arms to "restore Jews to their status of humiliation." But when I met him in his first-floor office after Israel's 2014 devastation of Gaza, his venom was directed at "the dictators of Islam" who had turned the faith into a xenophobic tyranny. He berated the

Saudis for closing Mecca and Medina, where he had studied, to
non-Muslims. Islam, he said, needed to cooperate, not clash
with other civilizations. The Quran, he insisted, denied access
only to "unclean idolaters" (9:28), not the People of the Book.
He cited an Ottoman imperial firman from 1564: "No Muslim or
believer in the unity of God should be hindered in any way if he
wishes to visit the Holy Cities and perambulate the luminous
Ka'ba." Ottoman Islamism, he says, could yet provide an inclusve
antidote to the religious exclusivism of the modern Middle East.

The Way Back: Jewish Perspectives

In 2048, when Palestinians mark the centenary of their Nakba, the first wave of refugees will be dead. Israel's leaders will likely reenact their victory against Arab armies who in 1948 advanced on multiple fronts, and celebrate a hundred years of statehood. Riot police will crowd Nakba memorials. But the greater the suppression of memory, the greater the wound. Far from fading, the unresolved contradictions Lord Balfour posed in his declaration of 1917 become more glaring as time passes: How can a Jewish homeland not "prejudice the civil and religious rights of existing non-Jewish communities living in Palestine?"

As long as a millet seeks exclusive control of land, not only of its community, as in Ottoman times, it threatens others who share that land. Before the 1967 Six-Day War ignited their messianic flights of fancy, national-religious Ashkenazis and

Sephardi traditionalists focused more on ther conmmunal role than conquest of land. They were the leading advocates of engagement with Islam and the ones most wary of turning a world religion into a land cult. "A bit more modesty, a bit less vanity and pride won't be unhelpful to us," Haim-Moshe Shapira, the leader of the national-religious party, was reported to have told Israel's cabinet after Israel's conquest of Sinai in 1956. He criticized Yitzhak Rabin, Israel's then chief of staff, for leading Israel into war in 1967, and was the only cabinet minister to oppose Israel's attacks on Palestinian guerrilla bases in Jordan. He supported a limited return of refugees and was an early champion of a land-for-peace agreement with the Palestinians. His model, he said, was Yochanan ben Zakkai, a Talmudic scholar and pacifist who negotiated with the Romans after the conquest of Jerusalem in 70 CE to secure a continued Jewish presence on Palestine's coastal plain.

Religious modesty soon succumbed to millennialism. Gush Emunim, the right-wing movement that grew powerful after the Six-Day War, interpreted Israel's conquests as a divine gift that men had no right to hand back. Land took precedence over people. Gush Emunim's students entered government, and Shapira's school dwindled, preserved only by a handful of religious human rights activists.

Shapira's values are once again gaining currency amongst some Jews as the religious settler movement expands into Arab locales. "Experience has helped us grow up," says a mature student at the yeshiva Israel's national-religious movement opened in the historically Arab town of Jaffa. He found more in common with the Arab translator and poet on his block

162   than his Jewish neighbors. "I feel our purpose is to find a way to live together, not to throw each other into the sea." Arab and Jewish residents in the south Haifa suburb of Ein HaYam (formerly Wadi Jamal) who initially feared the establishment of a *garin torani*, or religious "seed" community, would upset the neighborhood's relative harmony, express surprise at how engaged such religious societal groups are in building communal relations. Even on their West Bank hilltops, religious settlers have proved less rapacious than their secular forebears who settled the coastal plains. They build side-by-side with Palestinian towns, not atop their ruins, as the state's secular founders had done. "More threatening to me than the Jews crying 'death to Arabs' are the kibbutzniks who say they are pro-peace but stole our lands," says Jamal Zahalka, the most astute of Israel's Palestinian parliamentarians.

Perhaps the messianic exuberance awakened by conquest, too, might recede. As memories of the 1967 conquests mingle with successive retreats from Sinai, Lebanon, and Gaza, God's plans for Israel no longer look quite so one-directional. The two main ultra-Orthodox parties, United Torah Judaism (which represents Ashkenazi followers) and Shas (which represents those of Sephardi origin) both criticize the national-religious focus on one of the Torah's commandments, settling the land, while undermining their devotion to the other 612. Life is more important than land, they have ruled, and Israel should withdraw from the latter if it safeguards the former. They protest, too, when religious Zionists arrogate to themselves the ability to force God's hand. The temple will not be realized by disrupting Muslim worshippers at prayer in al-Aqsa Mosque, say ultra-orthodox rabbis, but rather descend, when the time comes, from heaven complete.

Surprisingly, given such dovish approaches, international mediators have shunned religious leaders and looked to secular actors to negotiate terms at contested holy sites. Understandably, they seem to believe holy sites are better dealt with as matters of legal conveyancing and real estate than as emotive touchstones that spark religious wars. Yet in sidelining religious leaders they risk jettisoning the flexibility of religious traditions and turning powerful religious movements into spoilers. Tired of waiting for invitations to peace talks, rabbis and imams are increasingly exploring alternative ways forward. Michael Melchior, a former chief rabbi of Norway and an Israeli parliamentarian, has sought to craft an alternative peace agreement with Hamas's former deputy prime minister, Nasr al-Din al-Shaer, an academic from Nablus who completed his doctorate at University of Manchester on attitudes towards women in Muslim and Jewish medieval texts. After years of backroom engagement, both of them tentatively went public to condemn attacks their own communities launched at the other's holy places. "Killing innocents on a religious basis violates the principles of Islam," protested al-Shaer after a gunman killed two Jews in an attack on Copenhagen's main synagogue in February 2015. None of Israel's Hebrew language press reported the unprecedented denunciation from a senior Hamas figure of an attack on a synagogue. "There are no votes in peddling peace," said Melchior, bitterly. "You get them from marketing hate."

Still undeterred, rabbis from the Council of Torah Sages, the committee that governs Shas, have devised their own draft

164   peace plan. To the consternation of secular nationalists in both the Labor party, and its sometime Palestinian counterpart, the PLO, national-religious Israeli parliamentarians have held meetings with their Palestinian counterparts from Hamas.Instead of focusing on an endgame, which only God can determine, they negotiate on the practicalities of a *modus vivendi*, which is for man to resolve. With the backing of their religious leaders, Israeli and Hamas negotiators met repeatedly under Qatari auspices in Doha, seeking to finalize an unfettered access agreement for the movement of people and goods into and out of Gaza, in exchange for a five-year cessation of violence. While doing nothing to reverse Israel's continued occupation of the West Bank, it could yet set in train a process for Jews and Muslims to share life, as well as land.

Milletocracy

"I acknowledge there is no God but God, and Abraham is the friend of God."
— engraving inside Jaffa Gate, the Old City of Jerusalem

"The European side," Sayyid Abu Musameh, Hamas's former leader in Gaza, proudly explained when giving me the directions to his new flat in Istanbul.

The address was a consolation of sorts. Though he had visited Britain and addressed a meeting at the House of Commons in 2005, ever tightening restrictions on proscribed organizations had barred him from the European Union thereafter. He had left Gaza in 2012, seeking both medical treatment and an escape from siege and despair. At least for the time being, Israel's cyclical offensives had rendered futile his repeated appeals for peace, not just between Palestinian and Israeli governments but between their peoples.

Instead he had joined other Islamists from across the region in devoting his energies to forming a parliament of elected members from across the Muslim world that one day, he hoped, might elect a caliph. Unlike Abu Bakr al-Baghdadi's tyrannical version, his newfound caliphate would be the product of elected representatives, something akin to the European Union. Undemocratic states would be barred. Non-Muslims could elect the caliph but not become one.

For all its shortcomings, Abu Musameh's neo-caliphate provided a framework for managing transnational sectarianism. Since the collapse of the Ottoman Empire, the region's regimes had struggled but failed to turn monotheistic religions—which were essentially universal in application—into stable nation-states. Despite or perhaps because of their brutal, sometimes milleticidal tendencies, each continued to arouse the opposition of other millets. By working within a region-wide framework, Abu Musameh reasoned, each millet would have no alternative but to balance and regulate its intra-millet relations. Instead of rival states, millets would regain their Ottoman role as part of a pan-regional alliance. If milleticide is the product of carving the region into sectarian states, milletocracy is its antidote.

Abu Musammeh's new order owes much to a past one. Under Ottoman rule, millets managed their communities, not territory. Each millet was autonomous, enforcing its own laws and raising its own taxes. Inasmuch as it was led by a religious leader whose religious courts applied religious law, it was a theocracy. But its powers were also extra-territorial, applying to all members of the confession regardless of their location. In that sense the millet's remit extended much further than the confines of the region's current regimes. The authority of the   chief rabbi of Istanbul stretched from the Nile to the Euphrates. Next to his reach, the Jewish settlers' aspirations for Greater Israel are myopic.

To Western powers and secular nationalists who attribute the region's murderous intent to its religious zeal, giving any more rein to the forces of sectarianism is anathema. The endemic wars of religion are ample testimony of how dangerous a force they remain. Yet with or without western blessing, religious leaders will continue to galvanize the region's masses and induce them to gird arms. Absent a mechanism for taming it, sectarianism will continue to wreak havoc region-wide.

Liberals will fret that the formalization of a confessional system will erode individual liberties. Yet the current approach scarcely offers better. For all their pretensions to guarantee personal liberties, even the region's most progressive regimes remained beholden to religious personal laws. In Jordan, Israel, and Lebanon, religious courts continue to prevent individuals from marrying outside their sect. Precedent would suggest, moreover, that once existential fears subside, religious leaders can display uncanny pragmatism. In Najaf, the hawza's newfound confidence has prompted long-cloistered and reclusive ayatollahs to open their shrines and seminaries to other faiths and engendered a new theology of inclusiveness, which amounts to a reformation. Should their fears of exclusion similarly ease, the region's Sunni clergy, too, might rediscover the traditions of tolerance and openness that for more than a millennium characterized Islam and ensured that caliphs and sultans—far more than their Christian counterparts in Europe—protected, preserved, and patronized the Middle East's plethora of ancient sects. If the Imam Ali Mosque shrine can open its doors to non-Muslims, so might Mecca one day. Reintegrated into the region, Sephardi rabbis might also recover their aptitude for latitude from a time when Muslims, Christians, and Jews shared the same shrines. In terms of tradition as well as theology, they might recognize that the current hostilities are an aberration.

Decades of accumulated vested interests will undoubtedly complicate the path back from nation-state to milletocracy. Governments will balk at surrendering their exclusive hold on territory, which for a century they have invested in holy attributes. Their education systems and media, which foster suspicion of other millets, have had a profound impact on the public consciousness. Reopening public space to other millets ostracized for decades will not come naturally to younger generations taught to fear and fight them.

But bereft of an answer to the region's problems other than conflict management, most of the regimes offer no vision for a more harmonious future, and many indeed only prime them for fresh bouts of conflict. Over time that lack of vision will drain them of support from a public that knows the region deserves better.

Foreign powers, too, desperate to see stability restored, know that reliance on the current crop of regimes is no better than a short to medium-term punt. In search of a respite from war, international mediators relaunch peace processes in fitful spurts in the almost messianic belief that they might deliver an elusive endgame. As in the past, they focus on border demarcation and partition as if all that eluded resolution was the right formula for putting the warring parties into separate boxes. Few stopped to ask whether the problem might be the paradigm itself, or ask the millets whether they really wanted to be boxed.

Rather than invest their efforts in engineering the right dimensions for, say, Israeli and Palestinian states, mediators might have greater success helping both parties break down barriers. Access and movement agreements that incrementally help lower barricades could do more to resolve conflict than talks on border demarcation that only build them higher.

Too often sidelined from negotiations, traditional religious leaders have a key role to play not only in mobilizing public support but also in bringing to the table the centuries of experience they have in successfully managing intra-millet relations. More concerned with preserving holy communities than holy land, they may be better equipped than politicians in devising ways of protecting the millet, while more equitably distributing resources and land. Across the region religious leaders have consistently opined that human life is more sacred than territory, and backed proposals that relinquish exclusive claims on land for genuine peace.

Holy sites are a case in point. While secular politicians and foreign mediators treat them as disputes over real estate, religious leaders can draw on past traditions of shared places of worship, and endorse their restoration of overlapping rites of worship. In Istanbul, local Muslim and Christian leaders have broached reconsecrating the Hagia Sophia, previously the seat of the Byzantine patriarch and favorite mosque of the Ottoman

170   caliphs, but not a drab godless museum. Beneath its dome, Muslims might again pray on Fridays, Christians celebrate mass on Sundays, and tourists visit the museum on other days. Religious leaders could also lobby for the reopening of traditional pilgrimage routes governments blocked when they sealed their frontiers. They should consider jointly tabling a proposal for Israel to let Muslims from Gaza and the West Bank pray at alAqsa Mosque, and for the Arab League to provide a safe passage for Israelis to access Jewish shrines in Egypt, Morocco, and the more stable parts of southern Iraq.

In the wake of increased religious traffic, other access and movement restrictions would seem anachronistic, too. Merchants could press for an end to sieges, boycotts, trade sanctions, and tariffs. The Arab League could leverage direct flights to Tel Aviv as the flip side of a package to lift Israel's closure of Palestine's air and seaports. A Lebanese entrepreneur could be encouraged to relaunch the Haifa-to-Beirut ferry service, taking Tel Aviv's clubbers to Beirut and bringing together Palestinian families separated for four generations. National railway networks study the feasibility of reopening the coastal railway that ran along the East Mediterranean coast from Alexandra via Palestine to Beirut. The possibilities seem fanciful, until one remembers how the region functioned in the past, when Lebanese travel agents printed their ski brochures in Hebrew.

Where religious leaders and merchants led, politicians could churlishly follow. As old social norms regained their footing, scare-mongering might lose some of its currency. Governments could experiment with reciprocal residency agreements, providing for Palestinian refugees to move across borders that

are currently closed. The old Jewish quarters of Beirut, Baghdad,
and Bahrain could slowly regain their old patrons. Jaffa would
again become an Arab economic and cultural hub, with cinemas
once screening Arabic and Hebrew films alike. The prospect of a
Middle East Schengen Agreement, providing for the unfettered
movement of people and goods across the region, as in Ottoman
times, would fall into reach.

A final step in the process would see the restoration of transnational millet rule. Local district councils would be entrusted
with managing municipal affairs, while pan-regional millet
leaderships would administer, regulate, and safeguard their own
confessional groups. With collective rights determined solely
by members of the millet, issues of comparative and combat-
ive demographics would lose some of their import. Jews could
remain a majority in their legislature, no matter how many
Sunnis there were, and would no longer need to place another
millet under military occupation to secure their existence.

Such a transformation is not a mere flight of fancy. Similar
ideas are already garnering traction. In 2010, a group of Israeli and
Palestinian experts drafted a proposal entitled "One land—two
states," providing for the creation of parallel Israeli and Palestinian
states "each covering the whole area" between the Mediterranean
Sea and the Jordan River and "decoupling the link between state
and territory." Under this model, Jews and Palestinians would
vote for separate parliaments but be free to live wherever they
chose. Amongst the parties to the 230-page document were
not only academics and artists but retired generals. (Curiously,
while looking to the future the initiators failed to mention the

172   historical roots: only a century ago the region operated on the
basis of parallel authorities holding sway in the same territory.)

Lebanon offers a foretaste of how such a system might
look. In 1989, Saudi Arabia needled the factions that had waged
a 15-year civil war—characterized by car bombs, Western
hostage-taking and civilian massacres—into signing the Taif
Agreement. The agreement distributed power among the
country's three predominant sects—Maronite Christians,
Sunnis, and Shias—giving each a formal role in government,
while leaving each to regulate its internal affairs. Twenty-five
years on, Lebanon, the most parlous and least populous Arab
state, has survived the turmoil of the Arab Spring better than
almost any other Arab state. Where previously regional rivalries
magnified internal divisions, wrenching the country's fragile
confessional matrix apart, under the Taif system the leaders of
each sect became stakeholders with vested interests in keeping the system intact. The collapse of one could have led to the
collapse of all. Pluralism was not a liberal luxury but a funda-
mental criterion of stability. While neighboring Syria collapsed
into sectarian bloodletting and drew in Lebanon's own sects,
Lebanon itself has largely ridden out the storm.

The Islamic State remains a threat and a thorn to the region,
but in historical terms it is a containable one. In many ways it
conforms to the regional norm of the past century. Across much
of the Fertile Crescent Sunni Arabs are also seeking to join the
regional club of millets that have turned into states. For all its
self-publicized barbarity, al-Baghdadi's caliphate butchery
compares favorably to that of the armies which carved their
own states out of the Ottoman Empire, and—despite their acts

of genocide and sectarian cleansing—still secured seats at the
UN. Even in its infancy, IS can claim to have instituted a more
tolerant system than its Saudi antecedents. It allows women
to drive, treats foreign Muslims as equals and not indentured
labor subject to the Gulf system of *kifalah,* or sponsorship, and
(unlike Saudi Arabia) still lets some Christians go to church.
"The safest place to be a Christian in Syria is in Raqqa," says a
Western ambassador monitoring the treatment of Christians,
with only a mild dose of irony. In areas under IS control,
extortion and hostage-taking have been stamped out, he
says. "The city's churches have been stripped of their icons,
but Christians are otherwise free to pray." Shiism might be
a heresy, but in accordance with *maslaha,* the sharia principle
of communal interest, IS still provides safe passage to Shia
truckers smuggling its oil and wheat. And the best antidote to
IS would be to address the communal grievances from which it
derives its strength. In a region prone to eschatological dramas,
emotions have a habit of subsiding as quickly as they flare.

The task of devising a Taif framework for the region might not
be as daunting as it appears. Though as seemingly hidden as
the twelfth imam, pluralism remains an ideal across the region.
The strange resistance of the region's governments to finally
demarcate their borders despite Western urging suggests too
that they are not as ready to definitively cut the Ottoman
umbilical cord as they sometimes profess. From Israel to IS,
the region's borders remain in a state of flux. Despite ample
opportunity to break away, Iraqi Kurdistan has yet to sever its
ties with Baghdad. Even Israel, which has done more than any

other state to divorce itself from the region, produces more Ottomanists—graduates of Ottoman history—than any other country bar Turkey. "Israel is not the island we sometimes think," says Miri Shefer-Mossensohn, a Tel Aviv Ottomanist. "Whether we like it or not, we are part of this region's past." Palestinians are no less nostalgic for the openness of Ottoman times. Before the imposition of siege walls, Gaza's port was Palestine's largest. There is much that still binds the region to its past. Given the right framework, sectarianism may yet be the sinew that pulls the region together—not the centrifugal force that wrests it apart.

When they erected the walls of Jerusalem, its Ottoman patrons had a notice engraved into the southeastern gate through which ran the road to Abraham's city, Khalil or Hebron. Rather than welcome travelers with the *shahada*, or testament, of one millet, Islam, it did so in the name of a prophet all the city's communities shared. "There is no God but God," read the engraving. "And Abraham is the friend of God." The sign is still standing. Few care to notice today, but perhaps one day more will.

Acknowledgments

Thanks first to Nicholas Lemann and Jimmy So of Columbia Global Reports for prodding me to write a book and seeing it through to fruition; my editors at *The Economist*, Ed Carr, Xan Smiley, and Anton La Guardia; Tim Fieldsend, who kept me from wandering, and Michael Sissons, my agent at PFD, for all his support.

Travelling is a wonderful way to experience that support system called humanity. I have been physically and spiritually nourished and housed by far too many to mention. The Middle East has lost none of its traditions of hospitality and can be a remarkably cheap place to travel.

The late Eyad Serraj was a political Houdini, hurdling the ghetto walls the region's armies have built around Gaza, even when losing the fight against cancer. He remains my moral compass. Bassim Naim, Mahmoud Zahar, and Husam Zumlot

176   in Gaza always outsmarted me in any argument, and taught me much in the process. Udi Eiran and Eliot Sacks did the same in Israel. I have yet to understand how Naftali Bennett can be such a warm individual and such a vicious orator. I still live in hope that he might one day correct himself. In another age Rabbi Michael Melchior would have been a prophet. I owe many insights and kindnesses to Makbula Nassar, Yazid Sadi, Lani Frerichs, Bill Van Esveld, Ana Uzelac, Rolly Rosen, and Mandy Turner. After Eyad, George Hintlian became my font of wisdom on all things Israeli, Palestinian, and Armenian. His company alone is worth a trip to Jerusalem.

Ara Sarafian and Ariadna Grigoryan made inspiring and generous travel companions through Western Armenia. Kerim Balcı prized open the world of the caliphate. Ghassan Salamé and Fareed Yasseen in Paris, Bassem Awadallah and Khalid al-Shammari in Amman, Anas Bouslamti and Mansour Malik in the Emirates, and Ezzedin al-Hakim in Najaf unwittingly shaped much of this book's thinking. I am indebted to them all, particularly to Ezzedin, who also gave me a wedding ring. Saad Salloum and Akeel Khuraifi are two walking genizas, who at great personal risk prevent religious bigots from burying Iraq's waning subcultures. Abbas al-Sarsai and Ali Salami provided exceptional company as they drove me round Iraq. Come the day when the Middle East sheds its walls I hope that they can all meet. They might just like each other.

Above all thank you to my family—Lipika, my wife, and Rishi, Sara, and Arun, my children—each of whom helped me filter the region through their different lenses, and made the journey all the richer by sharing it.

PART ONE

That the best books on the Middle East are about the past says much
about the state of the region. For a window into an Ottoman world, Philip
Mansel's two charming works *Constantinople: City of the World's Desire,
1453–1924* and *Levant: Splendour and Catastrophe on the Mediterranean*
remain unsurpassed in portraying the empire's haute culture, and help
explain why a century on such a benighted region continues to inspire
such love and nostalgia. Salim Tamari's *Year of the Locust: A Soldier's
Diary and the Erasure of Palestine's Ottoman Past* and Michelle Campos's
Ottoman Brothers both offer turn-of-the-twentieth-century descriptions
of how Palestine was so very different from the collection of xenophobic,
gated communities it is today. Louis de Bernières's *Birds Without Wings*, a
historical novel set in a southwestern Anatolian village, vividly depicts how
Ottoman pluralism unraveled and its people lost their innocence.

PART TWO

Two Israelis, one an urban planner and the other an architect, have
written remarkable accounts of how Israel relandscaped Palestine. Meron
Benvenisti's *Sacred Landscape: The Buried History of the Holy Land since 1948*
examines the changes Israel has made to the rural environment. Sharon
Rotbard's *White City, Black City: Architecture and War in Tel Aviv and Jaffa*
similarly exposes what lies beneath Israel's metropolis. Bruce Hoffman's
Anonymous Soldiers provides a sympathetic but very insightful account
of the role Jewish terrorists played in achieving statehood. *The Dove Flyer*,
a semi-autobiographical novel by Eli Amir and a powerful Israeli film,
portrays the painful transition from an Iraqi homeland to an Israeli one.

PART THREE

A splurge of recent publications depict the rise of Islamic State. *Under the
Black Flag: At the Frontier of the New Jihad*, by Sami Moubayed, a Beirut-
based journalist, has a wealth of background despite sloppy editing. *The
Syrian Jihad: Al-Qaeda, the Islamic State and the Evolution of an Insurgency*,
by Charles Lister, maps the plethora of Sunni groups that have converged
and competed to produce the rebellion against Bashar al-Assad. In *Heirs to
Forgotten Kingdoms: Journeys Into the Disappearing Religions of the Middle
East*, Gerard Russell, a former British diplomat, moves amongst the ancient
sects that had survived the ravages of time until the rise of the Islamic
State. He produced it just in time.

PART FOUR

Fanar Haddad's *Sectarianism in Iraq: Antagonistic Visions of Unity* is a colorful account of Iraq's descent into sectarian strife, brought to life by contemporary poetry. My *A New Muslim Order: The Shia and the Middle East Sectarian Crisis* is a record of the multiple new theologies that arose after America's 2003 invasion and continue to vie for dominance over Iraq's long-suppressed Shia. *Iraq: From War to a New Authoritarianism*, by Toby Dodge, shows how Saddam-like Iraq's post-invasion crop of Shia rulers became.

PARTS FIVE AND SIX

Charles Allen's *God's Terrorists: The Wahhabi Cult and the Hidden Roots of Modern Jihad* is a highly readable, finely researched historical account of the roots Saudi Arabia shares with al-Qaeda and Islamic State. *The Islamic Utopia: The Illusion of Reform in Saudi Arabia*, by Andrew Hammond, a former Reuters correspondent in Riyadh, offers a more contemporary account of how Salafis rule in Saudi Arabia, and might rule much in Syria and Iraq should IS survive. Penny Johnson and Raja Shehadeh have edited a highly compelling collection of essays charting the demise of the region's political order called *Shifting Sands: The Unravelling of the Old Order in the Middle East*. It is full of larger theories but also choice tidbits, including the revelation that France's negotiator François Georges-Picot signed the Sykes-Picot Agreement in ink, while the Briton Sir Mark Sykes used a pencil, reflecting each side's attitude towards the pact. For those who despair that diversity, humor, and art might survive the turmoil, this book is a delightful antidote.

180   ENDNOTES

PART ONE

25   **a new Turkish dam:** "New Dam in Turkey Threatens to Flood Ancient City and Archaeological Sites," by Julia Harte, *National Geographic*, February 21, 2014. http://news.nationalgeographic. com/news/2014/02/140221-tigris-river-dam-hasankeyf-turkey-iraq-water/

25   **once a tenth of the local population:** "The Ottoman Census System and Population, 1831–1914," by Stanford J. Shaw, *International Journal of Middle East Studies* 9, no. 3 (October 1978), p. 337.

25   **"blood-soaked depravity":** "Genocide of the Christians," by Tony Rennell, *Daily Mail*, April 17, 2015. www.dailymail.co.uk/news/article-3044292

29   **frequently went court-shopping:** Interview with Miri Shefer-Mossensohn, Chair, Middle Eastern & African History, Tel Aviv University, August 2015.

36   **"kill microbes":** "Death's End, 1915: The General Massacres of Christians in Diarbekir," by David Gaunt, in *Armenian Tigranakert/ Diarbekir and Edessa/Urfa*, ed. Richard G. Hovannisian (Mazda Publishers, 2006), p. 359.

40   **Though charier of dismantling the world's last major Muslim power:** *Year of the Locust: A Soldier's Diary and the Erasure of Palestine's Ottoman Past*, by Salim Tamari (University of California Press, 2011).

45   **an Islamic system was an essential prerequisite for the country:** *Pakistan: A Modern History*, by Ian Talbot (St. Martin's Press, 1988), p. 251.

48   **garish Las Vegas-style hotels:** "City in the sky: world's biggest hotel to open in Mecca," by Oliver Wainwright, *The Guardian*, May 22, 2015. http://www.theguardian.com/ artanddesign/architecture-design-blog/2015/may/22/worlds-biggest-hotel-to-open-in-mecca

48   **became a Hilton hotel:** "Mecca's changing face: Rejuvenation or destruction?," by Yazan al-Saadi, *Al-Akhbar*, March 5, 2014. http:// english.al-akhbar.com/node/18888

PART TWO

51   **Zionist fighters:** *Anonymous Soldiers: The Struggle for Israel, 1917–1947*, by Bruce Hoffman (Knopf, 2015).

54   **a third of the Palestinian population had lived in cities:** *Sacred Landscape: The Buried History of the Holy Land since 1948*, by Meron Benvenisti (University of California Press, 2002), p. 6.

61   **47 percent of Israeli Jews favor expelling Israel's Arab citizens:** "Survey: Most Israeli Jews Wouldn't Give Palestinians Vote if West Bank Was Annexed," by Gideon Levy, *Haaretz*, October 23, 2012. http://www.haaretz.com/israel-news/survey-most-israeli-jews-wouldn-t-give-palestinians-vote-if-west-bank-was-annexed.premium-1.471644

61   **"To defeat our enemies":** "Jewish Army in Israel," by Uri Blau, *Haaretz*, February 5, 2012. http://www.haaretz.co.il/magazine/1.1698256

61   **Hosting a highly publicized Bible study in his home:** Israeli Government Press Office statement, September 4, 2015. http://www.imra.org.il/story.php3?id=68297

63   **38 churches and mosques were attacked:** "Israeli extremists burn the church where Jesus multiplied loaves and fishes," by Celine Hagbard, IMEMC News, June 18, 2015. http://www.imemc.org/article/71984

74   **The broadcasting authority banned it:** The advertisement listing the children's names can be heard at https://www.youtube.com/watch?wv=qcTbMOabFhg.

PART THREE

77   **the grave of Izz ad-Din al-Qassam:** "Izz al-Din al-Qassam: prêcheur et mujahid," by Abdullah Schleifer, *Méditerranéennes/Mediterraneans* no. 14 (Spring 2010), and "Teacher, Preacher, Soldier, Martyr: Rethinking 'Izz al-Dīn al-Qassām," by Mark Sanagan, *Welt des Islams* 53, no. 3–4 (2013), pp. 315–52.

77   **the cemetery for sale to a private construction company:** "Israel sells cemetery with Al-Qassam's grave to a construction company," *Middle East Monitor*, October 21, 2014. https://www.middleeastmonitor.com/news/middle-east/14791-israel-sells-cemetery-with-al-qassams-grave-to-a-construction-company

78   **The Palestinian impetus for jihadi Islam has long been downplayed:** "The Palestine Effect: The Role of Palestinians in the Transnational Jihad Movement," by Thomas Hegghammer and Joas Wagemakers, *Welt des Islams* 53, no. 3–4 (2013), pp. 281–314.

79   **he joined the Muslim Brotherhood:** "'Abdallāh 'Azzām and Palestine," by Thomas Hegghammer, *Welt des Islams* 53, no. 3–4 (2013), pp. 353–87.

182   80   **Palestine headed the list:**
Azzam wrote two books about
Palestine: *Hamas: Historical Roots
and Charter* (1989) and *Memories of
Palestine* (ca. 1990).

89   **Ali and his sons were robbed
of the caliphate:** *Under the Black
Flag: At the Frontier of the New Jihad*,
by Sami Moubayed (I.B.Tauris, 2015),
pp. 6, 190.

91   **a devoted following:** *Under the
Black Flag: At the Frontier of the New
Jihad*, by Sami Moubayed, pp. 103–4.

96   **IS's English-language
magazine,** *Dabiq*: Issues of *Dabiq*
are available for download at
http://jihadology.net/category/
dabiq-magazine

99   **government-sponsored
conference in Baghdad:** Conference
was held at al-Rafidain Centre for
Strategic Studies, Baghdad, on
March 18, 2015; attended by the
author.

100   **too many to count:** Interview
with Susan Wolfinbarger, project
director of the AAAS Geospatial
Technologies Project, May 2015.

100   **the most lucrative source
of finance after oil:** "Countering
the logic of the war economy in
Syria; evidence from three local
areas," report by Rim Turkmani et
al., London School of Economics,
July 30, 2015, p. 33. http://www.
securityintransition.org/wp-content/
uploads/2015/08/Countering-war-
economy-Syria2.pdf

101   **"Let them steal our artifacts":**
"Opinion: Let them steal our
artifacts—we do not deserve them,"
by Abdel Rahman al-Rashed, *Asharq
al-Awsat*, March 12, 2015.
http://english.aawsat.com/2015/03/
article55342230/opinion-let-
them-steal-our-artifacts-we-do-
not-deserve-them

101   **its 2015 manual for women:**
"Women of the Islamic State:
A manifesto on women by the
al-Khanssaa Brigade," translated
by Charlie Winter, Quilliam
Foundation, February 2015. https://
www.quilliamfoundation.org/wp/
wp-content/uploads/publications/
free/women-of-the-islamic-state3.
pdf

102   **The head of Tajikistan's
counter-terrorism police unit:**
"Commander of elite Tajik police
force defects to Islamic State," by
Dmitry Solovyov, Reuters, May
28, 2015. http://www.reuters.com/
article/2015/05/28/us-mideast-
crisis-tajikistan-idUSKBN0OD1AP
20150528#tZaaxAGcAEUbxR3s.97

105   **a "tactical stalemate":** "U.S.
Aims to Put More Pressure on
ISIS in Syria," by Eric Schmitt
and Michael R. Gordon, *New York
Times*, October 4, 2015. http://
www.nytimes.com/2015/10/05/
world/middleeast/us-aims-to-put-
more-pressure-on-isis-in-syria.
html?_r=1

105   **200,000 Iraqis returned to IS-controlled territory:** Interview with Jana Hybášková, European Union ambassador to Iraq, November 2015, and interview with UN official in Gaziantep, October 2015.

PART FOUR

111   **hailed it a fatwa for jihad:** "Advice and Guidance to the Fighters on the Battlefields," The Office of His Eminence Sayyid Ali al-Sistani, February 12, 2015. http://www.sistani.org/english/archive/25036/

114   **struggled to satisfy their wives:** See http://english.bayynat.org/Jurisprudence/sex.htm

119   **the Al Saadun, a Sunni tribe from the Arabian Peninsula:** *The Emergence of Modern Shi'ism: Islamic Reform in Iraq and Iran,* by Zackery M. Heern (Oneworld Publications, 2015), p. 34.

120   **depleted their ranks:** Basrah Governorate Assessment Report, UNHCR, August 2006. http://www.unhcr.org/459ba6462.pdf

PART SIX

150   ***Toward a Christian-Shia Dialogue:*** *Nahu al-Hiwar al-Masihi-al-Imami,* by Lwiis Saliba (Dar Byblion, 2015).

Columbia Global Reports is a publishing imprint from Columbia University that commissions authors to do original on-site reporting around the globe on a wide range of issues. The resulting novella-length books offer new ways to look at and understand the world that can be read in a few hours. Most readers are curious and busy. Our books are for them.

globalreports.columbia.edu

FALL 2015

Shaky Ground:
The Strange Saga of the
U.S. Mortgage Giants
Bethany McLean

Little Rice:
Smartphones, Xiaomi, and
the Chinese Dream
Clay Shirky

The Cosmopolites:
The Coming of the Global
Citizen
Atossa Araxia Abrahamian

ALSO IN SPRING 2016

Outpatients:
The Astonishing New World
of Medical Tourism
Sasha Issenberg

Shadow Courts:
The Tribunals That Rule
Global Trade
Haley Sweetland Edwards